the cat care

handbook

the
cat care
handbook

**THE COMPLETE GUIDE
FOR A HEALTHY, HAPPY
AND WELL-TRAINED CAT**

Catherine Davidson

Quercus

Contents

Introduction

Cats, it is generally agreed, are remarkable animals. They can be as friendly and companionable as any dog, as entertaining as a talking parrot or as hypnotically beautiful as the most colourful of tropical fish. The British poet T.S. Eliot – author of *Old Possum's Book of Practical Cats* – summed up their attraction when he said, 'There is nothing in the animal world, to my mind, more delightful than cats at play. They are so swift and light and graceful, so subtle and designing, and yet so richly comic.'

The first chapter of this book unveils the secret life of the cat, explaining why they behave as they do, how you can tell what a cat is feeling from its body language, and why a cat's miaow can mean many different things. All cat owners benefit from understanding their cat more – and all cats will appreciate having an owner who understands them.

There are many reasons for choosing to share your home and your life with a cat. However, you should give serious thought to the proposition beforehand. This book aims to tell you everything you need to know before you bring your cat home. Chapter two, Choosing a Cat, will help to confirm that you are suited to cat ownership, and guide you through practical matters such as where to look for one, and what you should do to prepare your home for its new occupant. This chapter will

also help you decide what kind of cat is right for you. Every cat has a charm of its own. Some people love to observe and assist in the process whereby a kitten becomes a full-grown, independent animal. Some are drawn by the special, almost aristocratic lineage of a pedigree cat, and will only consider owning a cat that is a perfect exemplar of its breed. Other cat lovers take a charitable pleasure in offering a home to a grown animal that has ended up at a rescue centre. Most cat owners, whatever their initial motivation, come to appreciate the companionship that a cat can offer above all the other benefits. Research shows that owning a pet can reduce stress and increase a person's sense of happiness.

As for making your cat happy, it's not all that difficult to achieve. Cats are naturally contented creatures. But your cat's wellbeing is bound to be enhanced if you have given some thought to what makes a feline tick. Cats have physical, emotional and psychological needs, and it is part of your responsibility as a cat owner to ensure that those needs are met. This is the theme of chapter three, which explains what cats need in order to thrive in a domestic setting. If you know, for example, that cats like to get up high (a behaviour rooted in their wild ancestors' drive to find a place of safety from where they could survey their territory), then you will naturally want to give your cat access to a look-out perch. By the

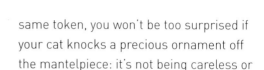

same token, you won't be too surprised if your cat knocks a precious ornament off the mantelpiece: it's not being careless or wilful, it's just following an ineradicable instinct. 'Thinking cat' in this way will enable you to provide your cat with the best possible environment, and will reduce the possibility of behavioural problems.

Chapter four deals with games and training. There is an idea – quite false – that cats can't be trained and that they are less intelligent than dogs. The fact is that cat intelligence is simply different, because cats are not programmed for life in a pack, in which cooperation and hierarchy are essential elements of the group dynamic. Cats live alone and for the most part please themselves, and so are less inclined to adopt the obedient modes of behaviour that we refer to as 'canine intelligence'. This independence of spirit – you might almost call it otherworldliness – is one of the most appealing things about the feline species. Nevertheless, your cat can be trained in certain ways that will make your life easier – to use a litter tray and a cat flap, for example, and even to walk on a leash.

The final chapter of the book is concerned with your cat's health. It contains important advice on how to deal with parasites, and how to safeguard your cat through procedures such

as neutering and vaccination. There is information on the other measures you must take to keep your cat healthy and hearty, and on how to pick up on the signs of illness and injury early on. As with human illness, many feline health problems can be resolved quickly if they are treated promptly. But your cat cannot tell you it is sick and, in fact, may even take measures to hide pain and illness when it occurs. This is another of those 'wild' behaviours, in this case intended to disguise any visible sign of weakness that might leave a cat prey to a rival or a predator. In a domestic situation, this dissembling aspect of cat behaviour can cause it needless suffering. It is therefore essential that you know your cat well, and that you watch out for any subtle signs that indicate it needs your help.

It's not hard to look after a cat, and it is very easy to love one. Follow a few straightforward, commonsense rules and procedures, and you will spend many pleasurable years enjoying your cat's company. A cat is an adornment for a house; every human generation since Egyptian times has known this. Today, people all over the world continue to invite these beguiling creatures to share the spaces where they live and the years of their lives. Cats are a kind of domestic inspiration. The French poet Jean Cocteau knew this well when he said, 'I love cats because I love my home, and after a while they become its visible soul.'

Cat behaviour

Cats, as every cat owner knows, are fascinating to watch, but much of their behaviour can seem inexplicable. Why, for example, does your cat rub up against your legs? Why is it always drawn to people who dislike cats? This chapter reveals the hidden meaning of cat behaviour, putting it into the context of the cat's wild ancestry. It explains how you can work out your cat's mood, and why cats groom and sleep as often as they do. There's also a brief history of the domestication of the cat, that mutually convenient and long-lasting contract between human and feline.

Understanding your cat is not merely interesting; it is a vital element of good cat care. If you know why your cat behaves the way it does, you will be better equipped to ensure that it has a satisfying and happy life in your home.

A history of cats

The domestic cat is known to biological science as *Felis catus*. It is the smallest and – to humans – the most friendly of an extended family that includes wild and predatory species such as lions, tigers, lynxes and leopards.

It has long been assumed that the ancient Egyptians were the first society to domesticate the cat – 4,000 years ago or more. Certainly there is ample evidence that cats were a feature of ancient Egypt, where they were revered above all other animals. The cult of the cat goddess Bastet endured as long as Egyptian culture itself.

The cat has never been held in as high esteem as it was in Egypt, but the pharaohs were not, in fact, the first cat lovers. Recent archaeological evidence suggests that humankind tamed the cat much earlier than had previously been supposed. In 2004, researchers on the island of Cyprus uncovered the remains of a carefully buried feline close to the grave of a Neolithic man. Both cat and man died around 9,500 years ago – some 6,000 years before the rise of Egypt. It seems reasonable to assume they belonged to

each other. Moreover, since cats are not native to Cyprus, some earlier migrants must have taken cats with them when they set out by ship from mainland Europe to colonize the island. They would not have gone to the trouble unless cats were in some way important to them.

THE FIRST CATS

The Cypriot cat is not even the earliest indication of an amiable association between feline and human. The new science of genetic sequencing has made it possible to trace the ancestry of living cats through their DNA, and so gain an insight into the

Left: **Some of the most beautiful ancient Egyptian artefacts are sculpted images of Bastet, sitting proud and alert in a pose that will be familiar to any modern-day cat owner.**

geographical origin of the population from which modern domestic cats are descended.

A study conducted in 2007 proved that today's cats are all descended from a group of wildcats that lived in the Middle East as long as 130,000 years ago. This is the time and the place when humans first began to grow crops in the area known as the 'Fertile Crescent'. The grain that those ancient sowers of seed stored for the winter would have attracted rats and other vermin. For the wildcats, those smaller mammals would have been easy pickings. It seems that cats elected to live in close proximity to humans because there was a ready supply of prey wherever people settled and made their villages.

Above: **The relationship between cat and humankind was at first symbiotic. Humans provided cats with food and a more secure environment; cats, for their part, kept rodents away from the winter grain stores.**

As for the humans, they were only too happy to welcome the felines, whose natural instinct served to protect their winter stores.

Both cats and humans have changed and developed since then, but many a farm cat today performs exactly the same function as its most distant domesticated ancestor. It seems certain that the relationship between the two species originated as a mutually beneficial arrangement, an unwritten contract that is still in operation after more than 4,000 human generations.

The garden predator

Anyone who has ever dangled a length of wool above a kitten has witnessed the early awakenings of the cat's predatory drive. A kitten will pounce at a moving target, and pin it to the ground as if its life depends on it – which, in the wild, it once did.

In adult cats, the call of the wild is expressed in a whole range of behaviours that come about entirely instinctively. Most cats will naturally stalk a bird or squirrel in the garden, and the urge is so engrained that they will do so whether they are hungry or not. You will sometimes see a cat fixing its gaze on its prey and swaying its head from side to side. This is its way of calculating distance, by looking at its target from two slightly different angles. Cats usually get only one chance to pounce, so it is important to judge the leap exactly.

In the event, most domestic cats rarely catch anything, due to a simple lack of opportunity. When they do succeed in catching live prey, they have the distressing habit of toying with it rather than dispatching it with a swift bite. This is the cat's way of prolonging the fun of a chase

Below: **Toying with prey often has a practical purpose. A larger animal, such as a rat, for example, may need to be stunned or it could cause the cat serious harm. Domestic cats also toy simply for the fun of it.**

Above: **Cats, like all their feline kin, are born hunters. The many millennia of domestication have not eroded the cat's killer instinct, nor has the past 150 years of selective breeding.**

– catching prey is such a rare event that the cat wants to make the most of it. Experienced ratters may also exhibit 'batting' behaviour: they will stun a rat with a couple of hard blows of the paw, so that it is too dazed to bite back, before going in for the kill.

IN FOR THE KILL

A vestige of the 'killer bite' instinct sometimes manifests itself when a cat spots a bird or some other prey outside a window. In these instances, the cat's teeth may begin to chatter in anticipation of killing its prey. This swift series of miniature bites is precisely the movement of the jaw that allows cats to drive their teeth quickly and efficiently into the spine of a small animal, and so end its struggle in an instant.

Claire's cat Cleo has started depositing dead mice under her bed. Claire is confused by this behaviour. Her cat isn't hungry, so why is she killing?

- -

The answer lies in a cat's maternal instincts. In the wild, a queen will bring prey to the nest: first dead prey, then live prey that she will dispatch in front of her kittens to teach them how to eat and hunt.

Cleo is doing the same for Claire as she would for her kittens. Giving Cleo more food won't stop the killing, nor will scolding her. All Claire can do is take the gift in the spirit it is offered, praise her cat for her efforts, and then discreetly dispose of the unfortunate prey. If she wants to alert potential prey to Cleo's presence, to give it a better chance of escape, she can fix a bell to Cleo's collar.

The sociable loner

Cats are programmed to live alone rather than in groups, but they do enjoy human company. These two instincts coexist more or less happily within every cat. That is their achievement, and it is the essence of domestication.

Most members of the wider cat family – with the exception of lions, who live in prides, and cheetahs and jaguarundis, who sometimes hunt in pairs – are solitary animals. Once cats are fully grown, they hunt on their own, they sleep alone, and they come together with other cats mostly to mate (or to fight over territory).

SOCIALIZATION AND KITTENISH BEHAVIOUR

In domestic cats, the instinctive loner behaviour has adapted and moderated itself through proximity to human society. Cats have learned to fulfil the human need for close companionship by preserving elements of their kittenish behaviour. Only a kitten would willingly submit to the amount of physical contact that grown domestic cats routinely experience from their owners – and then only from its mother. House cats, who perceive their owner as a mother-figure, experience human stroking in much the same way as they do their mother's grooming with her rough tongue.

The domestic cat's tendency to stick close to home is another example of infantile behaviour: the mature, wild instinct would be to explore far and wide. Purring is another manifestation of what might

Left: When a cat submits to the caresses of its owner, it is acting like a kitten being groomed by the rough tongue of its mother.

THE SOCIETY OF FERAL CATS

Not all domestic cats are domesticated. According to some estimates, almost half of the global cat population is feral – that is to say, they live close to humans but belong to no one. Feral cats are, in a sense, more social than domesticated cats. They can form colonies of up to 1,000 individuals. These massive groups are likely to base themselves in places where food is abundant and easy to obtain – close to a fish-processing factory, say. The feline desire for space and privacy is never entirely quashed, however. Each colony is divided into small 'gangs' of cats that identify with each other and maintain boundaries within the wider feral society. Although these societies can be large, the density of cat population may be significantly lower in these places than in a city suburb.

Below: **Self-reliance is one of the things that we humans – pack animals that we are – find so attractive and admirable in cats.**

be termed feline childishness, because the purr's main function is to act as a signal of contentedness from a kitten to its nursing mother. All these feline behaviours are enhanced by neutering, which has the effect of keeping cats at a more juvenile level of hormonal development.

Despite this socialization, the vast majority of the things that cats do during the course of a day are behaviours that they share with their distant cousins, the tigers and the panthers. Domestic cats – like all cats big and small – will groom their fur, prowl for prey, patrol the borders of their territory and, if unneutered, seek out opportunities to mate. In short, the natural behaviours of a wild animal are still very much alive in the pet cat.

The need for territory

All cats need some room of their own. In the wild, and in the countryside where space is not at a premium, cats can patrol a vast acreage. For most domesticated cats, however, territory is more limited and may be disputed.

Cats have a roaming instinct and a territorial instinct. They like to have a patch of land that they know belongs to them. The urge to stake out a claim to the land is rooted in the age-old competition for food – a cat's territory is its hunting ground, and every cat wants to keep its resources to itself. Although we humans now provide all the food that our cats need, every cat still wants its kingdom.

For indoor cats, this territory is easily defined: it is no more or less than the dimensions of your home. Two or more indoor cats that live together and know each other will happily share this cosy space, and need never encounter an aggressive neighbour or become embroiled in a border dispute. This is the comfortable life that most domesticated cats know in the USA and in Australia, where an indoor existence is the norm.

NEGOTIATING TERRITORY OUTDOORS

For cats that are allowed to come and go from the home – as is usual in Europe – territory is a rather more

Left: **Cats like to have a watchtower – a resting place in a tree or on a fence from which they can survey their domain and keep guard over it.**

fraught issue. All the cats in a neighbourhood need to come to a geographical consensus as to the 'ownership' of a particular turf. Remarkably, cats are extremely adept at settling for less individual territory whenever the density of the population is high – in inner cities, for example. That is not to say that territory is always divided equally. Males claim much more space than females, and neutered cats generally end up with less land than non-neutered ones.

A certain amount of feline diplomacy goes into these arrangements. Female cats often have areas of overlap in their territories which function as 'neutral zones', where they can meet without conflict. Females may also have to tolerate a dominant male who sees their territories as fiefdoms within his larger empire.

Territorial borders can shift and change if a new cat is brought into a neighbourhood and needs to carve out a stake for itself. Then there are feral cats, who are often no respecters of established borders, and have been known to pursue a

Above: **Cats in neighbouring or overlapping territories will tactfully avoid each other if they happen to be patrolling their mutual boundary at the same time.**

domesticated cat through its cat flap and into the home. As cats grow old, their territory shrinks – and when they die that inheritance has somehow to be redistributed. In such circumstances a feline turf war can break out.

BASIC INSTINCT **Marking borders**

Cats – especially unneutered males – have various ways of letting other cats know when they are trespassing. Chief among these is spraying urine. The pungent urine of a tom is an olfactory 'keep out' sign that he will regularly 'refresh' on his rounds of his territory.

Faeces send out the same signal – and sometimes defecating on another cat's territory is, for example, a deliberate, aggressive act on the part of a feral intruder. Cats also rub against various objects – a gatepost or a tree – to leave their scent at key points.

Movement and balance

Cats come in a range of shapes and sizes, but they are all built for the purpose of stalking, catching and killing smaller animals. To this end, millennia of evolution have sculpted a feline physique that is a natural essay in elegance.

FIT FOR PURPOSE

Cats are made for stealth, agility and swiftness. Everything about their body structure is honed, streamlined and purposeful. The skeletal system of a domestic cat is a bijou version of its bigger cousins, and is in many ways quite unlike ours. The collarbone of a cat, for example, is entirely detached from the narrow ribcage and is very small. The shoulderblades are also free-floating – held in place only by muscle and ligament. As a result, a cat's torso is highly compressible; it knows that if it can get its head through a gap, then the rest of its body will follow and not get stuck.

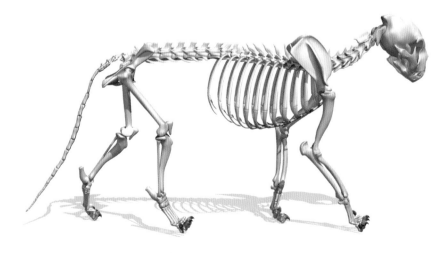

Below: **The skeleton of a cat is built to be robust and supple. It is designed for speed and manoeuvrability over the short distances that – generally speaking – are all it takes to catch a mouse or a rat.**

The spine of a cat is extremely flexible, and every one of the 20 vertebrae in the tail articulates like a many-jointed finger. This makes the tail a very subtle instrument. A cat walking along a narrow ridge can use its tail as a minutely adjustable counterbalance, like a tightrope-walker's pole. A cat's metatarsal bones (in its back feet) do not rest flat on the ground as they do in humans, and the metacarpals (the bones in the main part of human hands) do not form part of a cat's front feet. A cat walks eternally on tiptoes – silent, and always ready for a sudden leap or a burst of speed. It places each hindpaw directly in the print of the corresponding forepaw, minimizing noise and tracks.

The ability to make rapid movements is vital to a predatory species such as the cat, and it is facilitated by feline musculature. Most cat muscle belongs to a category known as Type II, which can burn up energy in an instant, but tires quickly. This type of muscle – combined with its flexible, springy skeleton – enables a cat to make prodigious leaps, and to chase prey at high speed (as much as 30 mph/48 kph) over short distances. More often than not, this is all it takes to make a kill. But if a cat misses its target, or does not catch its quarry in the first few seconds of a pursuit, then it has to stop to rest and let the muscles cool down. In effect, hunting cats gamble on getting it right first time.

BASIC INSTINCT **How cats fall on their feet**

The righting reflex of the domestic cat is legendary, and is what can allow it to survive a fall from a tree. It begins with the balance mechanism in the inner ear. The same apparatus that tells us we are on a pitching ship tells a cat which way is up or down. When a cat falls, it first turns its head groundwards, then twists the rest of its body into position. This is only possible because the feline spine is so supple. The tail acts as a stabilizer, keeping the cat level. If it has time and distance enough, the cat will spread its body to increase air resistance and slow its descent. Then, it will arch its back and extend its legs to absorb the shock of impact as it touches down – hopefully, without a scratch.

Cat
senses

Cats have all the same senses as humans – sight, smell, sound, touch and taste. But these basic capabilities are engineered in a uniquely feline way, and so a cat's perception of the world is very different from our own.

EYESIGHT

Cat vision is one of the marvels of nature. A cat's eyes, unlike a human's, are designed for darkness: they have a number of special properties that make it possible for them to see well – or well enough to hunt – in the dimmest of light.

The retina of a cat has a far higher concentration of 'rods' than

'cones'. Rods are 'photoreceptor' cells that work well in low light; cones are the cells that function best in bright light. At this most basic level, cats, by virtue of their rod count, have good night vision. The hours of dawn and dusk are prime hunting time, and they need to be able to see better than their competitors and their prey. The highest concentration of rods lies in a horizontal band across the centre of the feline retina, helping the cat to detect sudden sideways movements – like a mouse dashing for cover.

All other things being equal, a cat's night-vision is six times more acute than a human's. The trade-off is that cats are not as good at perceiving colour as daytime animals, because colour differentiation is a function of cone cells (although it is not true, as is often said, that cats are colour-blind). But there is more to a cat's keen night-sight than a

Left: A cat's eyes are designed to function well in low light, during the peak hunting times of dawn and dusk.

hypersensitive retina. Cats also have a layer of reflective cells, called the *tapetum lucidum*, which sits behind the retina. The tapetum reflects incoming light back through the rods, thereby making the retina doubly sensitive.

Like the human eye, a cat's eye reacts to changes in light levels by increasing or decreasing the size of the pupil. In humans, the pupil is always round and its size is controlled by a single muscle. Cats' pupils are controlled by a double muscle, like two sides of a curtain, that is much more versatile. It can narrow the pupil to a tiny chink in bright conditions – hence the characteristic vertical slit of a cat's eye – and in darkness it can open the pupil so wide that it almost fills the eyeball, allowing as much of the available light as possible to reach the retina.

Above: **Contrary to popular opinion, cats cannot see in the dark, but they can distinguish objects in dim light much better than we can.**

SUPERSENSITIVE HEARING

If cats had to rely entirely on their eyesight, they would still be fine hunters. But they have other equally useful weapons in their armoury. A cat's hearing is acutely sensitive, and even more acute than that of a dog. It can hear frequencies of up to 65,000 cycles per second. This is about an octave and a half higher than a human ear can detect, and it corresponds roughly to the highest-pitched squeak of a small rodent. More than that, a cat can swivel each of its ears through 180 degrees. Like radar dishes, its ears seek out the exact spot from which a sound has emanated. Cats can also hear sounds four or five times further away than humans can.

SMELL AND TASTE

A cat's sense of smell and taste is more refined than ours – although not as sensitive as a dog's. Like all animals, cats use smell and taste to check whether food is good or bad before they eat it. But cats, in common with many other animals, from tigers to llamas, have an extra organ that is used to part-smell and part-taste: the Jacobson's organ, also known as the vomero-nasal organ or VNO, which is located in the roof of the mouth on the hard palate. When a cat smells something, such as the urine of an intruding cat or the scent of a queen on heat, it will curl its lip into a strange grimace, known as the flehmen response. It 'laps up' the smell with its tongue to direct it to the VNO, which is connected directly to the hypothalamus, the part of the brain that governs anger responses and sexual activity.

FEELING THEIR WAY

When cats are moving around in the dark, they use their sense of touch to feel their way. The whiskers on the cheeks of a cat are a kind of hypersensitive motion-detection system. They are more deeply embedded in the skin than other hairs, and each whisker root is surrounded by a capsule of blood. Consequently, the slightest contact to the whisker, or tremor, is picked up and an alert signal is telegraphed instantly to the cat's brain.

Left: A cat will often appear to go into a kind of trance while it processes the fascinating chemical information supplied to its brain by the vomero-nasal organ.

Cats are magnificently equipped for their chosen lifestyle. They are primed to be at their best at dusk and in darkness, when their prey is active. They can use the combined power of their sight and their hearing to home in on a moving target that is almost made invisible by the night. They have their supersensitive whiskers and their special organ – the VNO – which tells them when they need to be on the defensive, and when a reproductive opportunity beckons. This all adds up to an impressive package, and it gives cats an edge in the eternal battle for survival of the fittest.

Above: **In pitch darkness, a cat will navigate its way using its hearing, sense of smell and its supersensitive whiskers.**

BASIC INSTINCT **Do cats have a sixth sense?**

Many cat owners have reported that their pets behave strangely ahead of some unusual or threatening event. It has been noted, for example, that cats (and other animals) exhibit odd behaviours before an earthquake.

In the Chinese city of Haicheng in 1975, the authorities evacuated the entire population because the animals were acting strangely – and a massive earthquake struck hours later. More spookily, there is a documented case of a cat named Oscar, who lived in a nursing home on Rhode Island and seemed able to predict when someone was about to die. When he curled up close to a patient, they usually expired a short time later. Oscar might have seemed psychic, but the more likely explanation is that he was attracted by a faint hormonal scent produced as the dying person's organs shut down. 'Seismo-sensitive' animals may detect gas emissions or micro-tremors that are too slight for humans to feel but which are nevertheless natural harbingers of an impending quake.

How cats communicate

Cats are capable of producing a surprising range of sounds, and research has shown that these noises are meaningful. They are a sophisticated way of sending signals to other cats – and perhaps even to us, their human companions.

The writer Lewis Carroll once remarked in jest that cats only make one sound, and complained that 'whatever you say to them, they always purr'. Charles Darwin, who had a rather more professional interest in animals and their ways, guessed that the vocal range of a cat amounted to half a dozen different utterances. Down the years, professional and amateur observers have attempted to put a figure on the number of significant cat noises – they range from 20 to 600. It has even been suggested that cats have an expressive language, complete with a grammar and a large vocabulary containing words for 'meat', 'mouse' and other concepts that loom large in the feline universe.

Below: **The caterwaul is heard when two rival cats come together, and often signals the beginning of a fight for access to a female on heat.**

VOCAL AGGRESSION

It is certainly true that there is more to feline vocalization than a handful of miaows and a purr. But the fact remains: cats can't talk. No animal can. However, like many animals, cats use sounds to express their mood and to communicate it to others. Take, for example, the caterwaul, a distinctive and exclusive cat noise. It is deployed whenever cats are angry or about to become engaged in a scrap, and this noise is often heard during the mating season, when toms are most likely to be in competition.

Vocal signs of aggression, from cats and many other animals, are used to give likely antagonists an idea of strength. He who growls loudest probably fights hardest; on hearing his opponent's signal, the weaker cat might well take note and back off before he gets hurt. In such situations, the caterwaul of the lesser tom might modulate to a slightly conciliatory guttural yowl. This sound expresses fear but does not entirely admit defeat; it is a kind of face-saver that says 'OK, you win this time, but think twice before you cross me again.'

HAPPY TALK

A more pleasant cat sound is the little rising trill known as the 'chirrup'. This sound is used by mother cats to summon her kittens, or to announce her return if she has been away from the litter for a while. Many adult domestic cats use the sound to acknowledge the presence of their owner who, as the provider, in the cat's mind is a kind of mother, and so triggers the sound appropriate to such encounters. For this reason, the chirrup is perceived by cat-loving humans as a greeting – the felinese word for 'hello', so to speak. The sound is also used when cats bring their owners 'gifts' of dead birds or mice. To a kitten, the chirrup in this instance would be a signal to pay attention to the hunting lesson to be learned; to humans the sound appears to mean: 'This is for you – because I like you.'

MIAOWING

Most day-to-day cat utterances can be classified under the broad heading of the 'miaow'. This sound is the adult version of the 'mewing' noise that kittens make almost from birth. In kittens the mew is a cry for attention, and the grown-up miaow is basically the same thing. That is not to say there are no gradations of meaning in the miaowing noise – far from it. Just as parents of small babies learn to understand the cries that their child makes – one might signal hunger, another that their nappy needs changing – so cat owners can learn to recognize the range of miaows articulated by their own pet. There might be a particular sound that your cat makes when it is expecting to be fed, another when it wants to be let out, a third when it wants to be stroked. Miaows are undeniably a form of communication between cats and humans but they cannot be said to amount to a cat language. They all boil down to the same message: 'Do what I need you to do, and do it now.'

Right: **Many owners report that their cats have a particular miaow when it is dinner time.**

PURRING

Of all the cat sounds, the purr is the most pleasant and soothing to the human ear. It is self-evidently an expression of feline bliss, but it may have other functions, too. It is an odd fact that cats sometimes purr when they are stressed, that queens purr when they are in labour, and that cats have been known to purr when they have been seriously injured. There is evidence that this kind of unhappy purring may have a therapeutic use. The particular frequency of a cat's purr may have the effect of promoting healing – possibly in a similar manner to the ultrasound techniques that are used in physiotherapy.

A new piece of research into cat purring, conducted at the UK's University of Sussex in 2009, suggests that some cats have learned to purr in a way that mimics the frequency of a baby's cry. The researchers termed this feline sound a 'soliciting purr'. It may be that its sonic similarity to the distress call of a human infant touches a deep nurturing instinct within humans, making the cat's

Above: **A purring cat is usually a happy cat, but not always. Cats may purr as a form of self-soothing when they are hurt.**

demands impossible to resist. If so, then the soliciting purr is an example of feline manipulation. Cats have adapted their natural behaviour so as to get the best (from their point of view) out of the humans who share their world.

BASIC INSTINCT **Why your cat rubs up against you**

Cats will often greet people who share their home by rubbing up against them. They will press their heads and their flanks against their owner's legs, and wind their tails around them. It looks like a kind of hello, a feline version of a friendly hug, and in a manner of speaking it is just that. But the point of the contact is not to express emotional closeness, as it would be with humans. By rubbing its head against you, your cat is daubing you with its scent, marking you down as a right-smelling member of its group (this is also what cats do to each other when they meet in the outdoors). Conversely, when it passes its flank along you, it is picking up your scent. You will notice that after greeting you it will immediately go off and groom its fur, which is how your cat tastes the human aroma it has just gathered and re-establishes its own scent.

Decoding the cat

Feline body language is highly expressive. The way a cat stands, the position of the ears and the manner in which it holds its tail are all indicative of a cat's mood and intentions, and its owner needs to know how to read these signals.

The meaning of a cat's behaviour is not always what you might suppose. Gestures that seem friendly may in fact be the opposite, and some actions can appear bizarre until you know what they mean. Cats are not four-legged humans; they are wild animals that retain much of their pre-domesticated nature. They see things differently from us. For this reason, it is a good idea for any cat owner to know something about the visual signals that cats give out. A little understanding of cat body language will make life less stressful for both feline and human.

Below: **This bristling cat is terrified, but hopes to fool an aggressor into believing it is bigger than it is by fluffing up its fur, arching its back, stretching out its legs and standing sideways on. It's a body-language bluff that often works.**

Feline posture can often be hard to fathom. A cat who is enjoying being stroked may arch its back in order to maximize contact with the friendly human hand. But an arched back is also the pose that classically signifies extreme fear or anger. In addition, if the fur on the back is bristling, then the cat is about to flee or (if it is desperate) to launch an attack. Sudden attacks can also occur when a cat is on its back having its belly petted. This is a highly submissive pose, and many cats will quickly grow nervous when their vulnerable stomach area is being touched. If the tail starts to twitch, that is your warning to stop – before your cat twists round and nips your hand.

THE WHOLE PICTURE

The body signals of a cat only really make sense when all the parts are considered together. The eyes, the ears, the tail and the pose are like words on a page – they each mean something on their own, but the message is much clearer when you have the whole sentence. When a cat stretches its head forward, it is generally a sign of greeting, but if the cat's head is lowered, you can't be so sure what it means. It may be a sign of aggression, or just as easily an indication of submission. The head is only part of the story. To be sure of the meaning, you need to take the position of the tail into account: a submissive cat will have its tail curled between its legs; the tail of an aggressive cat might be pointing stiffly at the ground.

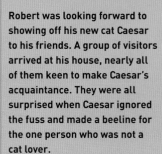

CASE HISTORY
Why cats like people who don't like them

Robert was looking forward to showing off his new cat Caesar to his friends. A group of visitors arrived at his house, nearly all of them keen to make Caesar's acquaintance. They were all surprised when Caesar ignored the fuss and made a beeline for the one person who was not a cat lover.

This behaviour is a classic instance of 'mistranslation'. Robert's visitors were all intent upon admiring Caesar and engaging with him, but in the cat world, direct eye contact, even in the form of an interested stare, is an aggressive act. So Caesar gravitated towards the sole individual who was not an apparent threat – the aloof visitor who was looking away. From Caesar's point of view, he was the one giving out the friendliest signals.

THE LANGUAGE OF EARS

The ears of a cat are highly mobile. Their movement is controlled by around 30 muscles (as opposed to the six we humans have), and they have evolved that way to help the cat locate prey in the dark. Their mobility means they can be a subtle indicator of the cat's inner state. A cat on yellow alert will slightly prick up its ears, although everything else about its demeanour will indicate that it is relaxed, or even asleep. A cat that is apparently asleep may track a suspicious sound with one ear – just as a preliminary precaution.

In an out-and-out conflict between two cats, the more frightened individual will flatten its ears against its head. This is a way of protecting a delicate part of the anatomy, but it also serves to send a submissive signal to the other cat. The aggressor will swivel its ears

Above: **The backs of the ears of the aggressor cat are visible during a fight, signalling that it is in control.**

sideways so that the backs are visible. This is a sign that he knows he has the upper hand, but it also allows for a swift switch to flattened ears should the defending cat find the courage to strike back.

WHAT THE TAIL SAYS

The tail is perhaps the most eloquent part of a cat's body, sending clear but complex messages to all cats and humans in visual range. A quivering, erect tail, for example, is a clear mark of pleasure, and is often displayed as a greeting. A swishing or wagging tail telegraphs anger or irritation. A tail that points straight up, but is hooked over at the top, contains a graphic hint that the cat in question is in two minds: friendly for the most part, but with some indecision or insecurity. Generally speaking, the higher a cat holds its tail, the more excited or content it is; a worsening mood manifests itself in a gradual lowering of the tail towards the ground.

Below: **Everything about this cat's body language shows that it is contented and alert: the body is relaxed and the ears are pricked.**

CHECKLIST
Tail talk

ERECT AND BRISTLING: extreme annoyance or anger

ERECT AND QUIVERING: affectionate or excited sign of greeting

TUCKED BETWEEN LEGS: submission to a dominant cat

SWISHING BACK AND FORTH: irritation or, occasionally, excitement

HELD HORIZONTALLY: neutral friendship, without suspicion

HELD UPRIGHT: friendly greeting

POINTING STIFFLY TO THE GROUND: determined aggression, on the point of attack

TWITCHING JUST AT THE TIP: alertness, and interest in events

CURVED DOWNWARDS AND UP AT THE TIP: relaxed and confident

Keeping clean

Cats spend many of their waking hours grooming their fur with their tongues. They do it first and foremost to keep the coat clean, but this archetypal feline ritual also fulfils needs that go beyond mere hygiene.

ALL ABOUT GROOMING

The self-grooming of a cat is a fascinating process to watch. Most have a fixed routine that they repeat two or three times a day. Their chief instrument is their tongue, the rough and spiny surface of which acts like a kind of comb. Cats generally begin by washing their face, using their paws and their forelegs to clean behind the ears, which is one of the few spots that they cannot reach with their tongue. They will work their way down their body – a cat is easily supple enough to lick its own spine – and finish with the tail.

The grooming process serves to brush out loose hair and any dirt or debris that has become attached to the

Below: **A cat may spend a third of its waking hours on grooming. It often follows a set sequence to help it ensure that every part of the body is cleaned.**

cat's coat. But it has other functions, too. The grooming process stimulates glands in the cat's skin so that they release waterproof oils into the fur, which help to keep the cat warm and dry. And a well-brushed coat naturally protects against enemies and the elements; it means there are no chinks in the fur armour that an enemy claw or a chill wind might penetrate. In hot weather, cats deposit saliva as they groom, which then evaporates and so keeps the animal cool. Sweat performs the same function in humans – but cats have very few sweat glands.

Cats will often groom themselves immediately after spending time in close contact with their owners. In this instance, they do it partly to taste your scent, but also to re-establish their own scent, which will have been 'contaminated' by human smells. And like many other more social animals, cats that live together will groom each other as a form of bonding. A shared scent is an unmistakable mark of belonging.

Furthermore, grooming can sometimes be performed for reasons

Above: Grooming serves as a displacement activity, which the cat engages in whenever it is feeling uncertain or agitated.

that are purely psychological. If, for example, a cat falls off a chair or a fence in plain sight of other cats or humans, it may settle down and wash itself. In this case the grooming is a displacement activity – it is the cat's way of communicating that its unfortunate slip was no big deal.

BASIC INSTINCT **Why a cat covers its faeces**

The fact that cats bury their faeces is often cited as proof of their cleanliness. In fact, burying faeces is the action of a submissive cat that wants to mask this most pungent odour – and so tone down its threat to others. Dominant toms in a feral colony or in the wild deliberately defecate in places where their faeces can be seen or smelt by other cats. This particular action is a display of territorial ownership, like a flag planted on a hill. Most domestic cats are submissive to their owners, and perhaps to other cats in the neighbourhood, and so the burying impulse is often to be observed in house cats.

Sleeping

Sleeping is a cat's favourite activity by far. Most cats sleep away a full two-thirds of their lives. This need for prolonged rest – like so many fundamental cat behaviours – is rooted in their wild ancestry, when downtime was essential for survival.

Sixteen hours' sleep a day is the norm for a domestic cat, but this is just an average. Various factors affect how much sleep a particular cat needs or wants. Feral cats and barn cats, for example, sleep a good deal less than house cats: by nature or necessity, they devote more of their time to hunting and defending their territory. Indoor cats sleep more than outdoor ones – perhaps because, given their secure and circumscribed lives, they have fewer things to worry about. Neutered cats also sleep longer than unneutered ones because they are not disturbed by the urge to mate. All cats sleep more in the winter than in the summer.

Newborn kittens sleep for as much as 20 hours a day, and ageing cats tend to sleep longer than younger ones. This is all perfectly natural, but bear in mind that unexpected changes in your cat's sleeping pattern can be a sign of illness. If your cat suddenly starts sleeping erratically, or far longer than usual, consult a veterinarian.

WHY SLEEP IS NECESSARY

Resting for long periods is the norm for carnivorous predators such as the cat. Lions do it, and so do unrelated meat-eating species such as snakes. A protein-rich diet means that such animals do not need to devote all their time to hunting for food (unlike many herbivores, which have to spend many hours a day grazing just

Left: **Kittens need their sleep, and will spend the majority of the day doing just that.**

to stay alive). Carnivores conserve their strength by resting, and they need this downtime to digest their prey – which itself is an activity that consumes energy. Domestic cats have retained these untamed habits. They sleep like hunters, although they no longer depend on the hunt for their survival.

At the same time, the cat generally sleeps very lightly – and this too is survival instinct. It is not unusual to see a cat sleeping with its

Above: **Your cat may sleep through continuous noise – such as the sound of a road digger outside – but awaken as soon as it hears you go into the kitchen. It can wake up in an instant if necessary.**

eyes half open, or with one ear alert and twitching. If disturbed, a cat can go from a state of sleep to total wakefulness in an instant. This is an obviously useful ability for a wild animal, which may have to escape a predator or stand and fight with an enemy at any moment.

DO CATS DREAM?

Although cats sleep for many hours, only about a quarter of their slumber time passes in the deeper mode of sleep known as REM sleep. REM stands for 'rapid-eye movement', and in humans is the phase during which we dream. If you wake a person during a period of REM, he or she will always be able to tell you what they were dreaming. Unfortunately, we can't perform that experiment with cats, but we do know that during REM sleep cats twitch their ears and flick their tails, their paws fidget, and their claws move in and out. All these signs indicate that cats, like humans (and, incidentally, dogs) process the experiences of the day by reliving them in their dreams.

The mating game

Feline courtship has customs and rituals all of its own. When the female is ready to mate, she summons the local toms with a distinctive high-pitched wail, and they, in turn, rush to be the first to mate with her.

Female cats become sexually mature at any time from four months to a year (the average is six months). Most domestic cats are altered (neutered or spayed) by the time they reach puberty. In a domestic setting, this is generally considered to be better for the cat and for its human companions – not just to forestall the arrival of unplanned-for kittens, which can be difficult to place, but because an unneutered cat is not particularly easy to live with.

WHEN A CAT IS ON HEAT

An unneutered adult female will come on heat every two to three weeks in spring or summer. The technical term for this cyclical event is *oestrus*, a Greek word which means frenzy or panic, and it's true there is an element of mad desperation in a female cat's behaviour at these times. She will be exceedingly restless and will yowl as if in pain. Her call is a highly distinctive sound, rather distressing to a human ear, and it is a signal to all the tomcats within hearing distance that the queen is desperate to mate. At the same time, she may crouch down with her hindquarters raised in the air and paw the ground as if she is walking on the spot: this is the sexually receptive pose known as lordosis.

Left: **A female cat that is ready for mating will raise the back half of her body upwards, holding the tail erect or to one side. She will call loudly for potential mates.**

Left: **A cat on heat is usually highly affectionate and may roll around.**

Many male cats can be attracted by a female's 'calling', and by the stimulating whiff of pheromones that accompanies it. If the female is accessible – in a garden, say – they will loiter expectantly close to her. Eventually the bravest of these suitors will sidle up to the queen – very gingerly, because she is more than likely to lash out viciously at any cat that approaches her too boldly. If she allows it, the tom will mount her, grasping the scruff of her neck in his teeth. This grip makes the queen remain still – the same triggered response that makes young kittens go limp when they are picked up by their mothers.

Copulation is extremely brief – a few seconds at most. It is a strange fact that the penis of a male cat is barbed, like a fishhook. The act of withdrawal therefore hurts the female, and often she will cry out and try to claw her partner. But it seems that the pain experienced by the female is a necessary part of the feline reproductive process, because it is the thing that triggers ovulation. Unlike other female mammals, cats do not release eggs until after they have mated.

The female will accept as many suitors as are on hand while she is on heat: she can easily clock up 20 or more encounters in a day. The female cat's only concern is to perpetuate her genes by producing offspring. As it happens, pregnancy almost always ensues from unrestricted mating. Sometimes a litter turns out to have multiple sires, which explains why the kittens may look very different from each other.

Mothers and kittens

Cats generally make good mothers. They know instinctively how to care for their litter. As for the kittens, they very quickly acquire the skills that they will need to get by in a hazardous world and may reach puberty after only a few months.

Cats give birth to a litter averaging three to five kittens about nine weeks after conception. Each kitten arrives with an interval of about half an hour. This delay gives the mother time to deal with each newborn in turn before the next arrives.

Below: **Each kitten feeds from the same nipple every time; the mother's nipples are 'labelled' as surely as if each one had its kitten's name on it.**

This first round of postnatal care is wondrous to behold. The mother uses her teeth to break the amniotic sac in which the kitten is delivered, then she cleans the newborn. She pays particular attention to the nose and mouth, so that these are unobstructed and the kitten can take its first breath. She bites off the umbilical cord and eats it. She also eats the placenta. (These will provide the mother with vital nourishment during the first hours and days of her confinement.)

Very soon, the kittens begin rooting around, looking for the mother's nipple. Remarkably, each of the mother's nipples is scented differently, and once a kitten has fed for the first time it will consistently return to the same one. This mechanism ensures that the kittens need not fight for food, and that none misses out for being weaker or slower than the others.

HOW KITTENS DEVELOP

Hearing and vision develops fast in the first weeks of life. By the time kittens are a month old they are running and jumping. They begin to exhibit hunting instincts in their play by chasing balls or indulging in mock fights. The mother may move the litter, one by one, to a new nest. It is not clear why cats do this, but it is probably connected to weaning, which occurs around this time: in the wild, the mother would be out looking for solid food for long periods, and would need to keep her litter in a place close to the hunting grounds.

Above: **Very young kittens may be cute, but for the sake of their health and sociability, you should wait until 12 weeks or so to remove them from the litter.**

By the age of two months, the kittens have teeth, they can see and hear perfectly well, and they are extremely nimble and playful. This is perhaps the time when kittens are at their most charming. Some cats retain this kittenish demeanour for many months but biologically they are already well on the way to adulthood. Some reach maturity as early as four months.

WHEN IS A KITTEN READY TO LEAVE ITS MOTHER?

Opinions vary as to the earliest age at which a kitten is ready for an independent life, but the general consensus among cat experts is that 12 weeks is a good moment. By that time a kitten will be weaned and litter-trained. The kitten will be socialized to a certain extent and it should be used to the sight, sounds and smells of the home. It should by now have been taken to the veterinarian for routine inoculations, and have been treated for worms. You should also by now have spoken to the veterinarian about having the kitten neutered. It may fall to you to have it done, or to the kitten's new owner. Either way, it should be borne in mind that kittens will reach puberty as early as four months and can have kittens of their own.

Choosing a cat

Cats make wonderful companions, and this chapter is all about helping you choose the right cat for you and your circumstances. For example, some breeds are content to be the lone feline in the house, while others crave a companion. Some cats relate well to children, while others most certainly do not. And some cats are better suited to an indoor life, but others will find it hard to cope without access to the outdoors.

Non-pedigree cats make good family pets, but you may like the idea of a cat that has a pedigree and belongs to a recognized breed. You may already know that you want a kitten, or that you prefer to give a home to an adult cat. This chapter covers all the options, and explains how to check that the cat you choose is healthy. It also tells you all you need to know about preparing your home for its new occupant.

Before you get a cat

Cats can live contentedly in most homes, so long as their basic needs for food, water, shelter and company are met. However, having a cat is a commitment that can last as long as 20 years, and you need to be sure that you understand what is involved.

Is your life relatively settled? This is the first question you should ask when considering cat ownership. Cats do not like change, so it is kinder to get a cat when your life is stable. If you live on your own and are often away on business, if you move home frequently – for example, if you are in the armed services – or if you plan to emigrate in the near future, then it's probably not the right time to get a cat.

MEETING THE COSTS

Cats are not expensive to keep, but pedigree cats usually mean a high initial outlay, and there are ongoing costs involved in caring for any cat. These include weekly bills for food and litter, as well as occasional expenses such as food bowls, toys and play equipment. Then there are fees for preventive healthcare, such as neutering your cat, as well as paying for annual check-ups at the veterinarian's, inoculations, parasite treatments and so on. You will need to make arrangements for your cat when you go on holiday, and this may involve fees for a cattery.

As well as the predictable costs, you need to know that you can meet veterinary bills if your cat has an accident or becomes ill. Take out pet health insurance, or place an equivalent amount aside each month in a separate bank account, so that you are covered for emergencies.

Left: **It's important to remember that regular check-ups, treatments and inoculations are all ongoing costs when you become a cat owner.**

PROVIDING CARE

Cats are known for their self-sufficiency but you will still need to dedicate some of your time to looking after them. As well as providing them with fresh water and suitable food each day, there are food and water bowls to clean and litter trays to change. Longhaired cats need daily grooming, and even shorthaired cats benefit from regular brushing. All cats need exercise, and some of this should come through playtime with their owner.

Ideally, one person will take on responsibility for ensuring that the cat is fed a proper diet and that it receives the correct vaccinations and parasite treatments. Don't rely on a child for this; although children often insist that they will care for an animal, few are able to do so, and they may lose interest once the novelty wears off.

OTHER ANIMALS

If you already own other animals, think about whether a cat can be integrated into the household. Cats can live contentedly with other animals, but the introductions need to be carefully managed (see pages 82–5). Slow introductions are important to minimize aggression and fear. Some animals, such as reptiles or a dog that is known to chase cats, will never make a suitable companion for a cat. Similarly, if you have smaller animals, such as rodents, fish, or birds, then you need to know that you can protect them from a cat, who will naturally view them as prey.

Below: **Cats and dogs are quite capable of coexisting peacefully, especially if they have been introduced to each other at an early age.**

OTHERS IN THE HOME

Not everyone enjoys having a cat around. Think about everyone who lives in your home, and check how each person feels about getting a cat. A house-proud person will not appreciate a cat that leaves hair on the soft furnishings (as almost all of them do). Someone who likes peace and quiet may find it difficult to coexist happily with a very vocal cat, such as an Oriental breed.

If anyone you live with has hay fever, asthma or other allergies, then he or she may also be allergic to cats – about 15 per cent of the population

Above: **Having an allergy shouldn't necessarily stop you from getting a cat, but requires thorough research into what measures will be involved in managing it.**

YOUR FELINE COMPANION

Cats can make remarkably rewarding pets and are known to offer both psychological and physiological benefits to their owners. Research has shown, for instance, that cats can help us to feel calmer and less stressed; simply stroking a cat can cause your blood pressure to drop and your heart rate to slow down.

The amount of petting a cat will enjoy or tolerate varies from cat to cat. Some of it is down to individual personality, but it also depends on the breed, and how much contact the cat has had with humans as a kitten.

Think about how much interaction you want to have with your cat before you choose one. Some people will find a very sociable cat such as the Siamese utterly charming, while others will find its demands irritating.

By the same token, if you will be leaving your cat alone for hours at a time, then you should choose one of the more independent breeds, such as a domestic shorthair. You may also want to consider getting two cats so that they can be company for each other.

are. The allergen is a substance found in cat saliva, which is deposited on the cat's skin and fur when it grooms, and forms part of the dander (skin flakes and secretions) shed by the cat. There are ways to manage sharing a home with a cat if you have an allergy, but you should research this thoroughly before going ahead (see also page 107).

If you have children, you will need to think about whether it is safe to introduce a cat. Young children may squeeze and hurt a cat, and the cat may scratch and bite. It may be best to wait until your children are old enough to treat an animal with respect. Check the personality of the cat carefully, to ensure that it gets on well with children; some breeds, such as the Abyssinian, are particularly known for their child-friendliness.

YOUR HOME

Consider whether you can offer a cat somewhere to live that is both safe and sufficiently stimulating. Cats like to have plenty of space to explore, although they do seem able to adapt to much smaller areas, and many cats live quite happily indoors (see pages 48–9). A tiny apartment, however, may not provide your cat with the space it needs to thrive.

Clearly, it's important to think about whether your environment is safe for a cat and to make the necessary modifications beforehand. For example, if you live in an apartment building, you may need to install protective mesh over your windows to prevent your cat from falling out.

Right: **As long as you take the necessary safety precautions, young children and cats can develop a strong, affectionate bond.**

Indoor or outdoor cat?

Cat owners differ in their opinions as to whether it is best to keep a cat indoors, or to give it access to the outdoors. Cats are naturally free-roaming creatures, but the outside world can be fraught with dangers for a domesticated animal.

In the USA, most cats are kept indoors – and the major rescue societies and most breeders insist that owners agree to this before they will place a cat with them. In the UK, by contrast, almost all cats are allowed to roam freely outdoors, as recommended by the major animal societies there.

There are reasons for this striking cultural difference. In the UK there are no natural predators such as coyotes, so the outdoors is safer. It is also argued that a higher proportion of Americans own pedigree cats, and these are more likely to be stolen. Pedigree cats are also less able to defend themselves against animal attackers.

NURTURING AN INDOOR CAT

Indoor cats live safer, longer lives, but they inevitably lead a less natural existence. You need to provide your indoor cat with enough stimulation and variety to keep it from becoming bored or stressed. This means toys to encourage exercise, as well as plenty of playtime with you. A scratching post is essential, ideally with a perch so that the cat can satisfy its urge to get up high (see page 93). If you have two cats, they will be able to amuse each other (see pages 52–3).

Left: Cats that are allowed to roam freely out of doors lead a more natural existence than indoor cats but inevitably are exposed to more risks.

If you decide on an indoor cat, choose one that has been reared indoors. It will display much less curiosity about the outside world than a cat who has already experienced it. Be sure to neuter your indoor cat. Neutered cats retain more kittenish personalities and adapt better to an indoor life than unneutered ones.

Right: **Play is an important way of releasing pent-up energy. Indoor cats need plenty of playtime to keep them amused and fit.**

CHECKLIST
The indoor cat

Pros

- 🐾 Your cat is protected from dogs and predators.
- 🐾 It is protected from cars, a major cause of death, and the possibility of climbing into an open vehicle and being driven away.
- 🐾 There is no risk of poisoning by consuming garden chemicals or eating poisoned prey such as rats.
- 🐾 Since indoor cats don't mix, they are much less likely to pick up diseases and parasites.
- 🐾 There is no need for your cat to engage in territorial disputes – with the inevitable injuries, and subsequent infections.
- 🐾 Your cat will not annoy your neighbours, or be at risk from anyone unscrupulous.
- 🐾 Your cat will not kill birds and small animals.

Cons

- 🐾 An indoor life is less stimulating – the smells, sounds and textures do not change.
- 🐾 Your cat is dependent on you to provide all its needs, including amusement and exercise.
- 🐾 It has less outlet for natural behaviours such as scratching and marking territory.
- 🐾 An indoor life offers little opportunity for social contact with other cats.
- 🐾 Your cat is more likely to become bored or frustrated, with resulting behavioural problems.
- 🐾 It may escape if windows or doors are left open, and is more likely to injure itself by jumping out of an upstairs window.

Kitten or adult?

When acquiring a cat, most people think first of getting a kitten. But adult cats have some distinct advantages over baby ones, and a grown-up cat may suit your lifestyle better, particularly if you do not have a lot of time for housetraining.

KITTENS

A kitten is hard to resist. It is fun to watch it grow up, it is naturally lively, and it adapts easily to your circumstances. However, a kitten, like all young animals, needs a lot of attention. It has to be fed several times a day since it has only a small stomach and needs plenty of nourishment. It has a natural propensity for getting into trouble, so

Left: **A young kitten is lovable, but will get into all sorts of mischief unless closely supervised.**

you will need to kitten-proof your home and keep the cat under close supervision. You'll also have to spend time training your kitten to behave – for example, teaching it to keep its claws out of the soft furnishings.

Your kitten will need plenty of love and attention, as well as frequent playtimes. If you have children, they will adore playing with a young kitten and seeing it develop. But a kitten is easily hurt if handled roughly, and will not be able to defend itself against a younger child who does not understand the cat's fragility.

ADULT CATS

There are many adult cats in shelters that need a loving home. Although not as cute as a kitten, an adult cat has its own advantages. For a start, it should be housetrained. It should have received its routine inoculations and been neutered, so your veterinary bills should be lower. It will also take up less of your time since it requires less attention and usually needs only two meals a day.

BASIC INSTINCT **Sexual matters**

Experts agree that all pet cats, male and female, should be neutered. An unneutered cat is not an easy house companion. A female on heat will yowl to attract potential mates – who may descend in large numbers on your home. A male will spray to mark his territory – which includes your property – and will fight to defend it.

So long as cats are neutered, the differences between the sexes are negligible. Many cat owners, however, claim a preference for male or for female cats. This tends to be based on past experience – which goes to show that both sexes can make good pets.

However, some people say that male cats are more loving, while female cats are often held to be smarter.

As your cat is already grown, its appearance and character are already set – you know exactly what you are getting. It may be less playful than a kitten, but this means that it is less likely to attack you or shred your favourite armchair.

It is worth bearing in mind that an adult cat may have behavioural problems, which can be hard to eradicate. A reputable breeder or shelter should disclose any known behaviour traits to you beforehand, and may be able to advise you on how to deal with them.

Below: An adult cat can bond with you just as well as a kitten, though it may take a little longer to bestow its affections and adapt to your lifestyle.

One cat or two?

Cats are known for their independence, but they are also very social animals. Two cats that live together can keep each other amused, so getting a pair of kittens from the same litter may be a good idea if your home is empty during the day.

Outdoor cats naturally come across other cats, and so can be quite happy being the sole cat in a household. Cats that live indoors, on the other hand, are isolated from other felines, and can easily become bored and unhappy. There are many ways of making their environment more stimulating, but the best way is often to provide them with another cat from the start.

TWO'S COMPANY

Most cats will be happier with a feline companion. They will play with each other, and be less likely to engage in destructive behaviour such as scratching your furniture. If you decide to opt for two or more cats, then the best way to do this is to acquire cats that are used to living together – ideally kittens from the same litter, or adults that have grown up together.

You can usually integrate kittens from different litters fairly easily, but settling two or more adults from different homes can be tricky. It is best avoided unless you are a very experienced cat owner since behavioural problems are almost inevitable. It is easier to bring a second cat into a home where one cat already lives than to settle two adults at the same time. An established adult cat will be more

Left: **An older cat may be irritated by a younger kitten's playfulness but won't usually be aggressive.**

Above: **Most cats will be happier with a companion, and two kittens from the same litter will usually get on with each other.**

tolerant of a kitten than another grown cat because the baby is less of a threat to its authority. It may also accept a cat of the opposite gender more readily. Bringing an additional adult into the home is hard but it can be done provided that both cats are relatively stable and social, and that the introductions are carefully managed (see pages 82–3).

Generally speaking, three or more cats are no more difficult to manage than two. But you need to be sure that you have the space and time to provide for each cat's needs. Bear in mind that your expenses will increase with each cat you have: the cost of buying food and litter could prove prohibitive if you have two, three or more cats.

CASE HISTORY
One cat too many

Jessica has always enjoyed having two cats, and when a friend moves overseas, she agrees to offer a home to his tom. The new cat adapts well, and happily spends long periods on Jessica's lap. Her female cat seems untroubled by the new arrival. Jessica's tom, however, takes to hiding out in her bedroom. Worse still, he starts to urinate on the bedcovers.

Jessica eventually realizes that the new tom has taken the position of 'top cat' in the home. He is also blocking her own tom's access to the litter tray – a common way for dominant cats to assert their power. So, her shy tom has had no choice but to urinate in his hiding place. When the situation fails to improve whatever Jessica tries, she reluctantly rehomes the new cat. Her own tom is instantly happier.

What type of cat?

Cats fall into one of three basic categories: pedigree, cross-breed or mixed breed. The major difference is often one of appearance, but there are also aspects of temperament and health to take into account before making your choice.

Cats have been selectively bred for less than 100 years, but there are now some 50 recognized breeds worldwide. Some of these are natural breeds, which have developed in particular areas of the world. Others have been bred to conform to a desired 'look', or to preserve a random mutation such as folded ears or taillessness. Cat breeders have deliberately cross-mated different breeds to create new and interesting coat patterns and colours.

SETTING THE STANDARD

Exacting standards for every aspect of a pedigree cat's appearance – its body shape, coat colour and pattern, eye colour and so on – are set by the cat associations with which pedigree cats have to be registered. If you want to show your cat, you should find out what these standards are. If a pedigree kitten does not meet them, it will not be suitable for showing but it can still make a beautiful house pet.

PEDIGREE CATS

Pedigree cats, by their very nature, are more varied than non-pedigree cats. They range from slender, sleek Orientals to the large, shaggy Norwegian Forest. If you buy a pedigree kitten, you know what it will look like as it develops. You will also have an idea of what its temperament is likely to be.

Below: **Pedigree cats such as this Maine Coon are a known quantity: you can be sure what you are getting in terms of its appearance and likely temperament.**

CROSS-BREEDS

Cross-breeds are the result of an accidental or planned mating between two different pedigrees. They can resemble one or other parent, or combine elements of both. Many delightful breeds were originally the result of a cross-breeding – the Exotic is a cross between a Persian and an American Shorthair, for example.

MIXED BREED

Non-pedigree cats, also known as moggies, are cats of mixed parentage. One or both of the parents may be a cross-breed, or they may be the result of a pairing between two non-pedigrees. Because the shorthaired gene is dominant, most non-pedigrees will be shorthaired. Provided they have been carefully reared, they have stable, well-rounded personalities.

CHECKLIST
What cat type is right for you?

PEDIGREE CAT
Pros
- Great variety in body type, coat pattern and coat colour.
- Predictable appearance: you know how the kitten will look when it is older.
- Known temperament, giving you a good idea of what to expect.

Cons
- Buying a pedigree cat is expensive.
- Some breeds have health problems. The breed you want may not be readily available.
- The cat may require large amounts of care and attention.

CROSS-BREED
Pros
- Great variety in body type, coat pattern and coat colour.
- Often hardier than pedigree cats.
- Less costly than buying a pedigree.
- More predictable in appearance and temperament than mixed breeds.

Cons
- May not be readily available.
- May have particular grooming or other care needs that are impractical for you.

MIXED BREED
Pros
- Generally hardier and healthier than pedigree cats.
- Inexpensive or free.
- Easily obtainable from various sources.
- Often available as adults as well as kittens.
- Large selection of colours and coat patterns available.

Cons
- Less controlled breeding, so harder to be sure the animal has been cared for properly.
- Difficult to predict how the cat will look as it matures.

Longhaired or shorthaired?

Cats are either longhaired or shorthaired. Most cat owners opt for a shorthaired cat because longhaired cats are harder work for their owners. If you are considering a longhaired cat, be sure that you know what is involved.

SHORTHAIRED

Most cats, including almost all non-pedigrees, are shorthaired. The gene that causes cat hair to grow longer is recessive, which means that it must be inherited from both parents in order to manifest itself in any given cat. This only occasionally happens in nature. Many longhaired breeds are 'man-made' – breeders produce them by introducing the longhaired gene into the bloodline of shorthaired breeds. The Balinese, for example, is a longhaired version of the shorthaired Siamese.

Shorthaired cats take care of their own coats, although a weekly grooming will help keep the coat tangle-free and glossy and will reduce the amount of shed hair on your soft

Left: **Whether you choose a shorthaired or longhaired cat may depend on how much time you have to spend on the grooming.**

CAT FUR EXPLAINED

There are three types of car hair: down hairs, awn hairs and guard hairs. Down hairs are usually short, fine and soft: they form the undercoat. Awn hairs make up the middle coat: they are longer than down hairs but shorter than the coarse guard hairs that comprise the top coat. Not all cats have all three types – for example, the Cornish Rex has no guard hairs, making its coat very soft to the touch. When the awn hairs are the same length as the guard hairs, the cat is described as 'double-coated'.

The wild ancestors of the domestic cat were all shorthaired. A short coat is practical: it offers protection from injury while being easy to keep clean and in good condition. Longhaired cats naturally occur from time to time, almost certainly as the result of a genetic mutation. Such events are so rare that the mutation does not usually leave a trace in the wider gene pool. But in the cold, mountainous regions of the Middle East and Central Asia, long hair sometimes conferred an evolutionary advantage. The mutation survived in the genetic makeup of some cats, and over the course of generations longhaired cats became established in the feline population at large. Such specimens were first brought to Europe as curiosities in the late Middle Ages. They were very popular in Victorian England, and they were exhibited at the first cat shows as 'Persians' or 'Angoras'.

Above: **A rexed cat has wavy fur, similar to that found in rexed rabbits. It came about as a spontaneous genetic mutation, and was then selectively bred.**

furnishings. If your time is limited, then a shorthaired cat is likely to suit you best.

LONGHAIRED

Persians – the most popular longhairs – require a long and rigorous grooming every day to remove loose hairs, and to prevent tangling or matting. If you want a Persian, you must be prepared to invest considerable time and effort in maintaining its coat. Some other natural longhaired breeds, such as the American Maine Coon, are largely self-maintaining and require only occasional grooming. If you have set your heart on a longhaired cat, but don't want a lot of maintenance, one of these cats may be a better option for you.

Coat patterns

Cats come with a variety of coat patterns. Understanding the terms used for these patterns will help you to work out if an advertised cat has the look you want, without having to go to the trouble of a visit.

Mackerel tabby: **Narrow vertical stripes on the sides of the body;** the stripes can be continuous or broken up into spots and bars. The legs and tail are banded (striped).

Classic or blotched tabby: **The sides feature distinctive 'bull's-eye' shaped whorls,** also known as oyster marks. The legs and tail are banded.

Spotted tabby: **The body and legs are covered with small oval or round spots.** Often the legs and tail are banded.

TABBY

The tabby is the most common pattern among domestic cats. This pattern features swirls, dots and stripes, and there is usually an M-shaped marking on the cat's forehead. There are four different tabby patterns.

Ticked or agouti tabby: **Each hair has light and dark bands,** creating a flecked 'salt-and-pepper' patterning. The legs and tail are usually striped though the Abyssinian has no banding here.

Solid or self: **A coat that is one colour** is known as solid in the USA and self in the UK. Kittens may have markings of another colour, but these should fade as the cat matures – if they don't, the adult cat will no longer be termed solid or self-coloured.

Bicolour: **A bicoloured cat has a white coat with patches of one other colour or patches of a pattern (for example, tabby).**

Van Bicolour: **A term used for white cats whose patches of colour are confined to the head and tail.**

Tortoiseshell or tortie: **A coat that is a mixture of black and orange patches, or their diluted colours of blue and cream.**

Brindled: **A coat that has random scatterings of colours rather than distinct patches. Tortoiseshell cats can be brindled rather than patched.**

Tricolour: **The term used for a tortoiseshell-and-white cat, which is also known as a 'calico cat' in the USA.**

Colourpoint: **A light-coloured body with darker 'points' (the face, paws and tail). This is the classic pattern of the Siamese cat, and is also referred to as 'pointed' or 'Himalayan' pattern.**

Sepia Pattern: **The face, legs and tail of this platinum Burmese are slightly darker than the coloured body. (Confusingly, the term is also used for the colour of the Singapura breed.)**

Mink: **Halfway between a sepia and colourpointed pattern, the body is coloured and the face, legs and tail are significantly darker. This Tonkinese has a mink patterned coat.**

Mitted: **Term used when the cat's feet are white – as in the Snowshoe.**

Coat colours

The range of terms used to describe cat colours is confusing. There are lots of words for variations on the same basic colours – and sometimes different words are used for the same colour in reference to particular breeds.

The rich language of cat colour is a matter of convention and long tradition amongst breeders, but from a genetic point of view cat colour is a relatively simple matter. There are four basic cat colours: black, chocolate, cinnamon and red. White cats are the result of all the genes for colour being masked in that individual animal: from a biological point of view they are technically 'colourless' or albino.

The vast variety of coat colours that you will encounter is the result of breeders (or nature) combining these four colours like a painter mixing oils on a palette. One simple way to vary the basic colours is to 'dilute' the gene, and so produce a paler version of the original colour. This process – sometimes known as 'maltesing' – has produced established colours such as blue (a dilute black), lavender (dilute chocolate), cream (dilute red), and fawn (dilute cinnamon).

Right: **Blue cats such as the Korat, Russian Blue and the Chartreux (shown here) are highly prized for their soft grey coats.**

Cat hairs are not always pigmented all the way along their length, and this circumstance can produce striking effects with coloured coats. If the hairs of a cat's coat are pigmented on the top half, but white underneath, then the white or cream will show through when the cat moves. This can be very eye-catching if the contrast between the topcoat and the undercoat is stark. These types of coats are termed 'shaded', or 'smoked' if the pigment goes almost to the base. A different effect is achieved if only the very tip of each hair is pigmented: the cat's coat appears to have a luxurious, almost metallic shimmer (this is termed 'tipped').

In the cat world, you will often hear the terms 'Eastern colours' and

Above: **This Persian cat's white coat is the result of the colour genes being masked.**

'Western colours'. Traditional Western colours are black, blue, red, cream and white; the Eastern colours are chocolate, lavender, cinnamon and fawn. It is perfectly possible to engineer Western colours into the Eastern group and vice versa – you can get British shorthairs in lilac or cinnamon, for example – but some associations do not recognize such transpositions in show cats.

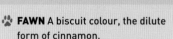

CHECKLIST
Glossary of coat colours

- **BLACK** JET BLACK, sometimes called ebony.
- **BLUE** BLUE-GREY, a dilute version of black.
- **CHAMPAGNE** A warm brown, equivalent to chocolate; used for Burmese and Tonkinese breeds.
- **CHOCOLATE** Warm, medium-toned brown, sometimes called chestnut.
- **CINNAMON** Light brown with a warm tone.
- **CREAM** Usually described as buff. Cream is the dilute form of red.

- **FAWN** A biscuit colour, the dilute form of cinnamon.
- **FROST** An alternative name for lavender/lilac.
- **LAVENDER OR LILAC** Pinkish grey, the dilute form of chocolate.
- **PLATINUM** Pinkish grey, equivalent to lavender/lilac; used for Burmese and Tonkinese cats.
- **RED** Professional term for ginger.
- **SABLE OR SEAL** Very dark brown, used to describe cats that are genetically black.

Gallery of pedigree cats

Cat breeds are hard to categorize because so many breeders take delight in introducing new and unusual variations. But there are some general groupings that can help you to narrow down your choice, and ensure that you pick the right cat for you.

Generally speaking, pedigree cats can be defined by body type and other physical characteristics. A cat's body type also gives an indication of the cat's origin, and can be linked to activity level. A long, lithe cat is likely to be more active than a stocky one.

ORIENTAL OR FOREIGN CATS

Cats that developed in the East developed long, slender bodies – giving them large surface areas that help to disperse excess body heat. The typical Oriental has a triangular-shaped head with large ears, long, slim legs and a long thin tail.

Oriental cats tend to be highly energetic, and it's often claimed that they are smarter and more trainable than other breeds. The Oriental is anything but a lap cat – if you choose an Oriental, expect your cat to be constantly on the go. Most Orientals, notably the Siamese, are loud and chatty. All Orientals are happiest in households where they receive lots of attention. They do best if given a feline companion, and should not be left alone for long periods.

Below: **The stunning Oriental Shorthair – a Siamese with all-over colouring – is demanding and highly vocal.**

NON-ORIENTALS

Cats that originated in the cold-weather countries have thickset, stocky bodies with large, rounded heads, sturdy legs and thick tails. Their shape is designed to allow them to retain their body heat. Typical breeds are the American Shorthair and British Shorthair, as well as the original longhaired breeds, such as the Persian, whose long coat is a natural defence against the winter.

Non-Oriental cats tend to be less active and less excitable than the Oriental cats. These cats usually have outgoing and affectionate personalities and tend to make companionable pets. As a rule, non-Orientals are more self-reliant than the Oriental breeds.

LARGE CATS

Compared to dogs, cats offer little variation in size. Attempts by breeders to produce much larger cats have been unsuccessful, and there seems to be a genetic limit on how big a cat can grow. That said, a few breeds are naturally hefty: a male Siberian can weigh nine kilograms (20 lb), double the average weight for a cat.

Large cats tend to be laidback and companionable. They are easy to train, and can enjoy playing games. The biggest cats – the Norwegian Forest, Siberian and Maine Coon – are longhairs. The Chartreux and the British and American Shorthairs are larger-than-average shorthaired cats.

QUIET CATS

Some cats are extremely talkative – a characteristic that can be endearing or nerve-jangling, depending on how you feel about cat chat. Fortunately, noisiness is one characteristic that is easy to predict in a breed. Particularly vocal cats include the Siamese, and its solid-coloured counterparts, the Oriental Shorthair, the Tonkinese, the Korat and the Devon and Cornish Rexes.

If you are looking for a quieter cat, then bear in mind that larger breeds tend to be less voluble: the British and American Shorthairs, the Persian, Exotic, Ragdoll and Maine Coon are all inclined to be taciturn. Other hushed breeds include the Chartreux, the Russian Blue and the American Curl. The Abyssinian is one of the quieter Oriental breeds.

LONGHAIRED BREEDS

The Persian is the cat that instantly comes to mind for most people when they think of longhaired breeds, but there are many other longhaired cats to choose from.

If you want a natural longhair, there are the large cats, such as the Maine Coon, and the more refined Turkish Angora and Turkish Van. In their attempts to produce ever-more interesting and appealing cat breeds, breeders have created longhaired versions of popular shorthaired breeds, such as the Somali (which is a longhaired Abyssinian) and Balinese (a longhaired Siamese). There are also some new longhaired breeds such as the Ragdoll and the Chantilly/Tiffany. The grooming needs vary considerably, from an occasional brush-through to a thorough daily combing.

The character of longhaired cats depends, as with shorthairs, on the body type – so the Balinese is active and vocal, like its relation the Siamese, and the cobby (compact, heavy-boned) Persian is calm and relaxed.

Above: **The Persian is the archetypal longhaired cat, and needs thorough grooming daily.**

OTHER FEATURES

If you want a cat that looks a little bit different, you may want to consider one of the unusual cats. These tend to be more costly, and harder to obtain, than other breeds, and there may well be long waiting lists for some of them. Most arose from a chance mutation, which was perpetuated by a canny breeder on the look-out for something new. They range from cats that have spotted 'wild-looking' coats, such as the Ocicat or Bengal; cats with bobbed tails or no tails at all, such as the Manx or American Bobtail; cats with curled ears, such as the American Curl; and strangest of all, cats that are furless, such as the Sphynx. If you want a cat with unusual characteristics, be sure that you research any potential health problems carefully.

ORIENTAL OR FOREIGN CATS

Siamese: **The beautiful Siamese is the most vocal and demanding of Oriental breeds.**

Burmese: **This companionable cat thrives on attention. Its playfulness makes it a highly entertaining pet.**

Tonkinese: **Highly popular in the USA, the Tonkinese is said to be one of the cleverest breeds.**

NON-ORIENTAL

British Shorthair: **The gentle, quiet British Shorthair is one of the most popular breeds in its native country.**

American Shorthair: **Breeds from cold-weather countries such as the USA have stocky bodies that help them retain body heat.**

The Exotic: **The Exotic is a shorthaired version of the Persian, and has the same calm temperament.**

LARGE CATS

Norwegian Forest Cat: **Affectionately known as the 'Wegie' for short, the Norwegian Forest Cat originated in Scandinavia.**

Siberian: **The Siberian is strong and agile – the gentle giant of the cat world.**

Maine Coon: **Popular in the United States, the Maine Coon loves to climb and play games.**

QUIET CATS

Russian Blue: **The handsome plush-furred Russian Blue is an affectionate and calm cat that is usually silent.**

Ragdoll: **Known for its docile character, the Ragdoll has a soft and melodious voice.**

Chartreux: **The Chartreux is less talkative than other cats, with a pleasing trill.**

LONGHAIRED BREEDS

Birman: **The Birman might be a natural breed, or a cross between the Siamese and Persian.**

Somali: **Sometimes known as the 'fox cat', the Somali has a ticked coat and playful personality.**

Longhair Selkirk Rex: **The Longhair Selkirk Rex is an eye-catching cat with a coat of thick loose curls.**

OTHER FEATURES

Ocicat: **The Ocicat has a distinctive spotted coat and was named for its resemblance to the ocelot.**

American Curl: **The American Curl is distinguished by its unusual ears that curl backwards in a smooth arc.**

Manx: **One of the most recognizable cats in the world, the Manx is known for having no tail.**

Where to get your cat

There are various places that you can obtain your cat, including breeders, friends, adverts and rescue homes. Choosing a reputable source will help to ensure that you get a healthy animal that is right for you – ask around for recommendations.

BREEDERS

The best place to get a kitten is from a reputable breeder. Your local veterinarian can usually give you details of breeders with good standards of care. Alternatively, a cat show may be a good place to seek out reliable breeders.

Generally speaking, a good breeder specializes in one breed or several related breeds. Cats from a good breeder are expensive, but are likely to be happy, healthy animals because they have been carefully raised. You may have to wait for your kitten, since breeders often sell at particular times of year, and will only place a kitten when it is ready to leave the mother.

You may also have to satisfy certain criteria before being allowed to purchase a kitten. Good breeders usually insist on the kitten being neutered, and may have other

Left: **A good breeder should allow you to observe the kitten in its litter, and to meet the mother cat. It's important to see the cats in their usual living environment.**

lifestyle requirements – for example, he or she may refuse to sell if your home is empty during the day, or if you plan to give the cat access to the outdoors.

PET SHOPS

It can be difficult to check the provenance and rearing conditions of a kitten sold in a pet shop. Often the kitten will have been disturbed by the change in its circumstance when it moves from the litter to the shop, and it may have had its socialization process interrupted. There is also a greater risk of infection, especially where many cats are kept close together. An increasing number of pet stores do not sell kittens for these reasons. Selling pets in shops allows for impulse buying, and cats shouldn't be bought on a whim.

CHECKLIST
What to ask a cat breeder

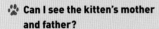

Can I see the kitten's mother and father?
You should always see the kitten with its mother, so that you can check she is healthy and of good temperament. You may also be able to see the father.

Can I see where the kittens live?
You should be able to check that their environment is suitable and clean.

Have the kittens had plenty of human contact?
Kittens handled regularly are more sociable than those who are not.

Have they been examined by a veterinarian?
The kittens should have had their first inoculations, and been given a clean bill of health by a veterinarian.

When will I be able to take the kitten home?
Kittens are ready to leave their mothers at about 12 weeks of age, though some breeders like to wait longer.

How long has the owner been breeding?
You want an experienced breeder, who is knowledgeable about the breed and its history.

Does the breeder show his or her cats?
Breeders who show generally have a passion for their animals, rather than seeing them as purely commercial products.

Are there any conditions attached to having the kitten?
There usually are.

Are there any hereditary defects in this breed?
A good breeder should be able to explain any congenital health problems and say how he or she is working to eliminate them.

Can I bring the cat back if it does not settle, or if it falls ill?
Usually you will be able to return a pedigree kitten if unforeseen problems develop.

Above: **A cat may be offered for adoption because the owner's circumstances have changed and he or she can no longer care for the animal or, less appealingly, because it has a behavioural problem.**

ACQUAINTANCES AND ADVERTS

Many people have obtained much-loved cats from a friend or neighbour, or via a newspaper advert. Notices put up in a local veterinarian's are a possible source, with the advantage that the staff may know the cats and their owner.

Non-pedigree cats offered in this way are generally inexpensive, or free to a good home. Such a cat comes with no guarantee of good health, and you should check that the mother cat's inoculations are up to date, and that both she and her litter look healthy. It is also a good idea to have the cat seen by a veterinarian before you agree to take it on.

Adult cats that need rehoming can make excellent pets, but to avoid getting a cat with unreformable behavioural problems, always find out why it is being given away.

What to ask a rescue centre

- **Where did the cat come from?**
  If it is a feral cat, it may find it hard to adapt to a domestic environment.
- **Does it have any known behavioural problems?**
  A cat may be handed in to a shelter because of soiling or another problem. Older cats are more likely to have behavioural problems than younger ones.
- **Is the cat healthy?**
  Cats should be checked over by a veterinarian, inoculated and treated for parasites before being placed.

- **Have you assessed the cat's temperament?**
  The shelter should be able to tell how the cat gets on with other cats, dogs and people. It may have done some socialization training that will help the cat settle in a new home.
- **How will you help me find a cat to suit my needs?**
  You should talk to a member of staff about your needs, your lifestyle and your home.
- **Will you help me if I have problems in the future?**
  The shelter may continue to offer behavioural advice after you have taken the cat home.

RESCUE HOMES

A reputable rescue home is an excellent source of adult cats. The staff should know the cats well and be able to match you with a cat of the right temperament.

Shelters can be run by national charities or by small local concerns. Some are better than others, and a poorly run rescue centre can disseminate infection. Check that the animals are housed in clean conditions, kept warm and well fed, and are able to exercise. The best reason for going to a rescue centre is that you are giving a home to an animal that would otherwise stay in an institution, or even be destroyed.

Below: **Some pedigree cats may be available from shelters, though most of the cats available are non-pedigree.**

Choosing a healthy cat

However you source your cat, make sure that it is healthy. Don't be tempted to get a poorly cat, which is likely to cost you a great deal in veterinary bills and emotional distress. Check it over to make sure it looks fit and well before you bring it home.

THINGS TO LOOK FOR

Watch the cat walking around, and check for lameness. Then pick it up and place it on your lap so that you can give it a thorough examination.

Be sure that the coat looks clean and smooth, and that there are no bald patches. Run your fingers over the belly – particularly if you are checking a kitten – to make sure it is not distended and there are no bulges. Be wary of any discharges from eyes, ears, mouth or anus, or for excessive scratching or headshaking, which may be a sign of parasites.

If you are getting your cat from a breeder or rescue centre, then it will usually have been checked by a veterinarian and given a clean bill of health. If this is not the case, ask if you can take it to a veterinarian for examination. You should be able to take a kitten or cat back to the breeder or rescue centre if it falls ill soon after you take it home, but always check this beforehand.

INFECTIOUS DISEASES

Your veterinarian will be able to check for the presence of infectious diseases such as feline leukaemia virus (FeLV), which undermines the immune system and can trigger cancer. It is passed from cat to cat, so it is essential not to bring a cat with FeLV into contact with others until you know it is free of the disease. Cats over six months can also be checked for feline immunodeficiency virus (FIV), the feline equivalent of HIV.

SIGNS OF GOOD HEALTH

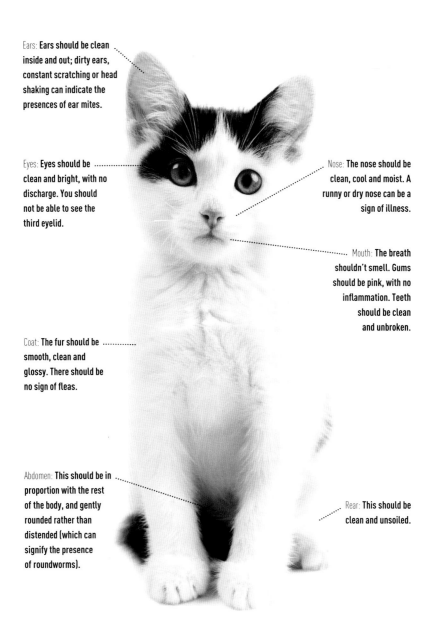

Ears: **Ears should be clean inside and out; dirty ears, constant scratching or head shaking can indicate the presences of ear mites.**

Eyes: **Eyes should be clean and bright, with no discharge. You should not be able to see the third eyelid.**

Nose: **The nose should be clean, cool and moist. A runny or dry nose can be a sign of illness.**

Mouth: **The breath shouldn't smell. Gums should be pink, with no inflammation. Teeth should be clean and unbroken.**

Coat: **The fur should be smooth, clean and glossy. There should be no sign of fleas.**

Abdomen: **This should be in proportion with the rest of the body, and gently rounded rather than distended (which can signify the presence of roundworms).**

Rear: **This should be clean and unsoiled.**

Choosing a happy cat

Physical health is only one aspect of a cat's wellbeing. Its temperament is also important. A short acquaintance is usually enough to get an idea of how sociable and happy a cat really is, and whether it is suitable for you.

If you are choosing a kitten, then it is best to choose one that has been handled regularly from an early age. Otherwise, it is likely to shy away from human contact later on. Kittens benefit from spending time in their litter, so don't be tempted to take a kitten that is much younger than 12 weeks. Some breeders keep their kittens for 14 or 16 weeks, because they feel the cats benefit from a longer period in the litter.

Below: **A kitten that has been well cared for will generally be curious and willing to play.**

Always ask to see the whole litter. Notice how the mother reacts to your presence – if she is relaxed and allows you to handle her kittens, that indicates her kittens will be sociable, too. Spend time playing with the kittens and see which ones are approachable and playful. Usually there will be a mix of personalities in the litter. Think about what level of activity will suit you: a very shy kitten may be hard to integrate into your household, while a highly playful kitten may prove too much of a handful.

BASIC INSTINCT **The toy test**

When you go to see a litter of kittens, take a couple of suitable toys along with you, such as a piece of string and a ping-pong ball. Once you have chosen a likely kitten and taken it away from its siblings, place it gently on the floor. Place your string or other toy in front of it and gently tease the kitten with it. A normal, healthy kitten should be playful and eager for the chase, and have plenty of energy to pounce, chase and bat its 'prey'.

ASSESSING PERSONALITY

When a particular kitten draws your eye, pick it up and take it away from its playmates. Do the toy test (see box) to see how it responds. Then spend a little time petting and cuddling it, and check that it seems to enjoy this. If it keeps squirming away, then it could be a cat that is too active (or fearful) to enjoy petting. If you want a companionable pet, then this cat may not be right for you.

If you are getting your kitten from a rescue centre or other source, you may not be able to see it in its litter, but you can still 'personality-test' the individual kitten. If you are choosing an adult cat, the person caring for it should be able to give you an idea of its personality and whether or not it has any behavioural problems that have led to it being given away. However, you should still spend time holding and petting it to see how it reacts. Ideally, it should be relaxed and responsive.

Below: **A happy kitten will enjoy human contact, so spend some time stroking and cuddling it to see how it responds to your touch.**

Preparing your home

Before your cat arrives in your home you will need to spend some time ensuring that the environment is safe, and that you have provided for its needs. There are many domestic hazards, from toxic plants to small spaces where a kitten may get stuck.

It's up to you to ensure that your home is a secure and reassuring place for your cat to live in. Kittens, like children, seem to be able to seek out trouble, so you should go from room to room, looking for hazards and making them safe. Adult cats, too, will need to be shielded from harm while they get used to your home.

DOMESTIC HAZARDS

Look for small spaces that your kitten or cat could crawl into (such as behind the refrigerator), and block them off. A cat can easily get inside washing machines, tumble dryers – and even ovens, so you must keep the doors of such appliances firmly closed. Shut cupboards securely, and invest in safety latches of the type used to keep young children safe. Keep lids on your bins so that your cat can't fall into them – use ones with foot-pedals if possible, as these are catproof.

Cats love jumping up high, so for the time being remove fragile ornaments from mantelpieces and shelves. Temporarily tie up drapes so

that your cat cannot climb them, and tie the cords of any blinds. Electrical flexes have irresistible appeal for kittens or playful cats, who may chew on them. Bundle them up or use cord containers. If you have an open hearth, it is essential to keep a fireguard in place even when the fire is unlit to prevent kittens getting stuck in the chimney. Other common dangers for cats include household detergents, and also houseplants such as amaryllis, ivy, philodendrons and poinsettias, which are toxic (see page 79 for more details).

Below: **A chimney is an enticing escape route for a kitten, so needs to have a fireguard in place.**

If you have sewing equipment in your home, keep needles and pins in a secure container. Cotton reels are favourite toys for cats, and they won't notice a stray needle until it is too late. Open windows in high-rise accommodation are another danger. Protect your cat from a nasty, even fatal, fall by fitting window screens.

THE SAFE ROOM

To help your new cat get used to your home, and to keep your kitten out of mischief, it is best to create a 'safe room' where it can spend the first days and weeks. This should be a warm, self-contained environment, containing the cat's bed, litter tray and feeding station (kept well apart from the litter tray) and some toys.

The best safe room is a bathroom, where you can clean up any accidents easily. Make sure the toilet lid is always kept down as a kitten could fall into the bowl and drown.

Above: **Your cat has a natural instinct to get up high, so it is best to put away fragile ornaments to prevent breakages.**

CHECKLIST
Essential equipment

Before you bring a cat into your home, you will need the following items (see chapter three, Basic Cat Care, for more details on each):

- Litter tray and litter scoop
- Litter
- Food bowl
- Water bowl
- Cat food
- Cat basket or bed
- Cat carrier
- Brush or comb

Preparing the garden

You can't entirely cat-proof the outdoors, but you can reduce the amount of hazards in your garden. Certain plants, ponds, neighbourhood dogs and cats, and garden chemicals can all pose a threat to your cat's safety.

The most effective way to ensure that your cat remains safe is to enclose your garden so that your pet cannot get out, and other animals cannot get in. One option is to surround your garden with high fencing (at least 1.8 metres/6 ft high) with a top that curls inwards to prevent cats climbing over. Overhanging branches from nearby trees will need to be pruned back to prevent their use as an escape route, while you should stop your cat from climbing any trees in the garden by blocking access to the lower branches

with wire mesh or suchlike. Make sure that you have your neighbour's consent if necessary and that you are abiding by any planning laws.

Alternatively, you could build a self-contained cat enclosure. This gives cats access to the outdoors without allowing them to roam free. Ideally this would be accessed from the home, but you could also include a purpose-built cat house so that your pet can shelter from the elements. Do bear in mind that if you enclose your garden, you are limiting your cat's territory and must therefore make sure that there are places where it can climb, perch, hide, play and sleep. You also need to provide a private latrine area.

SAFETY MEASURES

Do not allow a young cat unsupervised access to a garden containing a pond or swimming pool,

Left: **Block access to trees in your garden or lop off lower branches to prevent your cat from using them as an escape route and to stop other animals from getting in.**

since it could fall in and be unable to get out. Similarly, cover water butts and weight down the lids. Keep garden chemicals locked away – slug pellets, rat poison, wood preservatives, pesticides and many other garden products are poisonous to cats. Make sure that your cat cannot access garden sheds or garages, and that sharp garden implements are well out of reach.

PLANTS

Many plants are toxic to animals: these include clematis, azaleas and sweet peas. Adult cats do not usually eat poisonous plants, but a kitten or young cat may be curious enough to do so. If you are getting a kitten, you may want to remove the most toxic plants from your garden. Your veterinarian can advise you on this,

Above: **If you intend to let your cat outside, you will probably want to install a cat flap so that it can come and go as it pleases.**

and the Feline Advisory Bureau (www.fabcats.org) and the Cat Fanciers' Association (www.cfainc.org) publish full lists of plants that are dangerous to cats.

PROTECTING YOUR OUTDOOR CAT

Any cat allowed access to the outdoors should be vaccinated against common infectious diseases such as feline leukaemia. Your cat should also be

neutered – unneutered females are obviously likely to become pregnant, while unneutered toms travel much greater distances, which is likely to involve crossing roads. They also fight more than neutered ones, which places them at greater risk of infections.

Keep your cat indoors at night, when it is more likely to be hit by a car than during the day. It is essential that your cat is identifiable in the event that it gets lost or is involved in an accident. Your cat should wear a cat collar with an identity tag attached, and should also be microchipped (see page 97) – make sure your contact details are kept up to date.

Bringing your cat home

Cats dislike change, and there are few changes as great as leaving the litter and moving to a new home. Be sure you devote enough time to the settling-in process, so that the transition is as smooth and gentle as possible.

The journey to your home may well be frightening for your new cat because most don't like cars. It is important to make the experience as reassuring as you can. Firstly, be sure to transport your cat in a carrier – it is not safe otherwise. Take someone with you so that one of you can keep the carrier steady; place it on a seat secured by a seatbelt. Drive slowly, avoiding excessive braking. Cats often urinate or defecate when travelling, so line the base of the carrier with an old towel or newspaper. Stay with the carrier at all times; do not leave a cat in a car in hot weather.

SETTLING IN

When you reach home, take your cat in its carrier straight to the safe room (see page 77). Make sure that all doors and windows are closed, then open the carrier door and allow the cat to come out in its own time. Sit quietly nearby.

Give your cat some time to explore, then if it seems curious, hold out your hand and call its name but do not pick it up yet. If your cat wants to hide, let it do so. Visit the safe room frequently, speaking softly and moving slowly while you are there. Feed and play with your cat at regular times. If possible, introduce other people in the home only when your pet has gained its confidence with you.

Left: **Speak reassuringly to help keep the cat calm while it is in the carrier.**

After a few days – or even longer if your cat is nervous – leave the door to the safe room open so that your cat can explore the rest of the home. Always keep the door open so it can retreat when it wants to. When your cat is comfortable with its new home, you can move the bed, feeding station and litter tray to their permanent position.

GOING OUTDOORS

Do not let a new cat outside for at least three weeks, and supervise the first outings until it knows its way around your garden. A kitten should be supervised outside until it is six months old. If you decide to let a cat out on its own, it's a good idea to do so when it is hungry – that way, it is likely to return quickly for its meal. Be sure that it has a collar and identity tag and that it has been microchipped; your cat should also be vaccinated.

Above: **Put the cat carrier in the safe room in your new home, and allow the cat to come out in its own time.**

CHECKLIST
What to tell your children about a new kitten or cat

- Always be gentle.
- Do not keep picking the kitten up – allow it to come to you in its own time.
- Speak softly.
- Don't make sudden movements.
- Play gently – for example, by letting it pounce on a piece of wool.
- Respect the cat's mood – let it sleep if that is what it wants.
- Do not touch the cat's litter tray, or its food.

When cats first meet

Your cats are about to meet. A poor introduction can trigger an aggressive relationship between them that is hard to change, so it is important to set up the best conditions for an acquaintance, and let your cats get to know each other in stages.

Bring your new cat into the home at a time when there are no other disruptions going on – for example, festive seasons, overnight visitors or major redecoration. This means your resident cat should be relaxed, and that you will have time to spend on managing the process. Have your new cat checked over by a veterinarian to ensure that it is healthy first.

Remember that cats will get on best if they do not have to fight for your attention or over resources – cats usually need their own feeding bowl and litter tray. Generally speaking, kittens are less of a threat to adult cats than another adult, and a cat of the opposite sex may also be more acceptable to a resident cat.

INTRODUCING BY SCENT

In the wild, cats communicate largely by scent, and this is the best way to let your resident cat 'meet' the new arrival. Place the new cat in a safe room (see page 77), to keep the cats separate. Give each

Left: **It's normal for cats to have an occasional spat, and kittens enjoy 'fighting' as part of their play.**

of them plenty of affection and attention. Stroke one cat and then go to the other without washing your hands, to mingle their scents.

After a day or two, allow the new cat to explore the rest of the home while the resident cat is in another room (with the door closed). Continue to allow them separate access to the rooms of your home for a week or so.

THE FIRST SIGHTINGS

Then, give them their first sight of each other. The safest way to do this is to place the new cat in a carrier and put it above floor level, so that the two cats do not make direct eye contact. Let your resident cat discover the new one in its own time. Expect a bit of hissing and glaring, but distract the cats from overt signs of aggression by making a noise. Remain calm and praise more accepting behaviour, giving titbits to

Above: **You may need to feed your cats in separate places if one steals the other's food.**

reward them. Make extra fuss of the resident cat.

Do this several times, then progress to feeding them when they are near each other – the new cat in its carrier, and the resident cat outside. This can take days or weeks, depending on the cats involved.

When you judge the time to be right, let them meet without a carrier. Do this in a room where one or other can hide or get up high if necessary. Use food as a distraction, feeding first the resident cat, then the new cat. Stay calm and reward the behaviour you want. If all goes well, you can start to allow them to spend longer periods together – or you may need to continue to keep the new cat separate for longer. Be patient; most cats learn to get along in the end.

Introducing a cat to a dog

They may be proverbial enemies, but cats and dogs often live together quite happily. The introduction can be easier than that of two cats, but it still needs to be handled slowly and carefully when you first bring them into contact with each other.

Cats and dogs may be suspicious of each other at first, but they are not competitors, and most will make friends after a while. The same principles apply as when introducing two cats (see page 82): let the animals become aware of each other's presence through scent before proceeding to a face-to-face meeting.

As you would when introducing cats, start by using the safe room system, so that the cat is held in a confined area. Mingle the animals' scents by stroking one, then the other without washing your hands. You can also give the cat the dog's blanket to explore, and then pass it back again.

INITIAL CONTACT

For the first meeting, make sure the dog has been for a good walk and has been fed, so that it is calm. Place the cat in a carrier and put it on a high

Left: **Cats and dogs can get on very well, and the dog usually comes to see the household cat as part of its 'pack'.**

surface, then bring in the dog on a leash. Allow it to sniff the carrier, then get your dog to 'sit', and praise it for doing so. Give both cat and dog titbits as a treat, and keep the meeting short.

Repeat these visits frequently, until both animals remain calm. Then, allow the cat out of the carrier, but keep the dog on the leash. Control it with the leash if it shows any signs of bolting towards the cat, and allow the cat to dictate the level of interaction.

When you judge that the two animals are comfortable with each other, allow meetings with the dog off the leash. Make sure that there are high places the cat can escape to if necessary. Stay close and control the dog with voice commands. Gradually increase the length of the visits.

It can take a long time for an excitable puppy or a breed such as a terrier to learn to leave a cat alone. Keep your patience, praise the dog for good behaviour, and remember that if the cat makes a sudden dash,

Above: **The basic rule when introducing cats and dogs is to keep the dog firmly under control, and let the cat decide the amount of interaction.**

giving chase is a natural response on the dog's part – so be ready for it.

Be sure to keep the cat's litter tray somewhere the dog cannot gain access to, because it may eat the cat's faeces. For the same reason, place the cat's feeding bowl somewhere high up, out of the dog's reach (cat food is bad for dogs, and cats do not like to share their food). Both animals will usually prefer to have their own private sleeping space.

BASIC INSTINCT **Cats and smaller animals**

Cats are natural predators – and small creatures such as birds, mice and fish are the prey. You cannot overcome this basic instinct, so do not try. However, there are steps you can take to keep your other pets safe. House small animals in secure cages that your cat cannot access; cover fish tanks, and keep the door to the room closed when you are not around.

Basic
cat care

Cats have a reputation for being easy to care for, and
by and large that is true. They are self-reliant animals,
designed by nature to fend for themselves. Your cat's
wild ancestors had to find their own food and water,
defend their territory, find a safe spot to sleep and
choose a place to relieve themselves. A modern
household cat has a pampered life by comparison. It
doesn't go hungry and is protected from predators.

But since you are providing for your cat's needs, it
is essential that you understand what those needs are.
This chapter gives you the key facts about cat diet,
toileting needs, grooming and other aspects of cat
care. There's also special advice on caring for cats that
are kept indoors – as increasing numbers now are. All
this will help to ensure that your cat has a contented
and healthy life, and that you live happily together.

Toileting needs

Cats are fastidious when it comes to toileting, and often have a preference for a particular type of litter tray. You may need to experiment before you find one that suits your cat, and if you have more than one cat, each will need its own tray.

The litter tray is an essential piece of equipment. Even if you let your cat outside during the day, it should have a litter tray to use at night and to discourage it from relieving itself in neighbouring gardens.

There are two basic types of litter tray: open and covered (hooded). An open tray works well for many cats, and is inexpensive. It is made of sturdy plastic so is hardwearing and easy to clean. Some open trays have a rim, which helps to keep the litter from being scattered over the floor. You can also get disposable cardboard trays, which are useful if you are travelling with your cat.

The covered tray is preferred by many owners because it contains odour well, and also prevents any litter spill. It offers more privacy so can be a good choice for cats that are timid. However, some cats will not use a covered tray because it can become smelly, or because they find it claustrophobic. Covered trays may also be too small for large cats, and they are unsuitable for cats with asthma because they are not sufficiently ventilated.

Left: **Some cats prefer a covered litter tray, which helps to contain odours, but others do not like to be in an enclosed space and will be much happier using a simple open tray.**

Below: **It's important that your tray is big enough for your cat – if there isn't enough space for your cat to turn, it may well do its toileting elsewhere.**

Another, more high-tech, option is an electronic self-cleaning tray, which automatically rakes the soiled litter into a waste receptacle which you can empty later. A sensor activates the raking process some minutes after the cat gets into the tray, leaving enough time so that there is no danger of the raking starting while your cat is relieving itself.

TOILET TRAY ACCESSORIES

As well as a litter tray, you will need a slotted scoop so that you can lift out the used litter. You may also want to buy some plastic tray liners to make cleaning out the litter tray easier. If your cat doesn't like the feel of plastic, or if you prefer a more eco-friendly solution, newspaper is a cheap alternative. Place a sheet of newspaper or a mat under your tray, too, to prevent your cat from tracking litter throughout your home.

TOILETING TIPS

Choose a tray that is the right size for your cat. There should be enough space for your cat to turn around, and to use the litter tray more than once without getting soiled. The tray should be deep enough to contain enough litter for digging. Bear in mind, however, that kittens and elderly cats need a shallow tray that they can get in and out of easily.

If you have more than one cat, you should get at least one litter tray for each; one tray per cat, plus one extra is a useful formula. Many cats are happy to share, but having alternative trays means that nobody has to wait or use a tray that has been soiled. Don't put the trays in a row or one cat may 'guard' them all.

If your home has several floors, you should have one tray on each floor. This is especially important if your cat is elderly and cannot manage the stairs easily, or if you have a kitten.

What litter?

There is a bewildering range of cat litter available, and cats may get on better with one than another. Choosing the right litter for your cat is a matter of trial and error, but usually cats prefer finer litters, which are more comfortable for their paws.

It's important to remember that your choice of litter ultimately rests with your cat. You may prefer a scented litter to mask the odour of the tray, but if your cat won't use it, you will have to try a different type.

Whichever litter you choose, make sure you fill the tray to a depth of around five centimetres (2 in) to ensure that the cat can cover its faeces. Choose a dust-free, unscented variety if your cat has asthma.

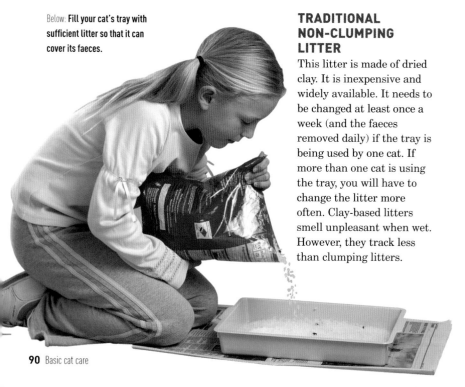

Below: **Fill your cat's tray with sufficient litter so that it can cover its faeces.**

TRADITIONAL NON-CLUMPING LITTER

This litter is made of dried clay. It is inexpensive and widely available. It needs to be changed at least once a week (and the faeces removed daily) if the tray is being used by one cat. If more than one cat is using the tray, you will have to change the litter more often. Clay-based litters smell unpleasant when wet. However, they track less than clumping litters.

Above: Clumping litter is often preferred by cats – and also by owners – because you don't need to change it as often as non-clumping litter.

CLUMPING LITTER

Clumping litter is made mainly of small grains of clay that stick together when wet. The used litter clumps can be scooped out of the tray easily, together with any faeces. Cats like the fine texture of the litter, and owners generally prefer it because it means emptying the tray less often than non-clumping types.

Clumping litter is more expensive than non-clumping types, and the litter can stick to the cat's paws and be tracked across the floor. Some vets advise against using clumping litter with young kittens because it may cause blockages if ingested.

SILICA GEL LITTER

This is the most absorbent of litters and it eliminates odour almost completely. You remove faeces from the tray daily, but only need to change the litter when it becomes

saturated (every four weeks or so). Silica gel litter is much lighter than clay-based litters.

BIODEGRADABLE LITTERS

Litters made from corncob, hemp and other recycled or renewable resources are more environmentally friendly than conventional litters. You can get both clumping and non-clumping varieties. Biodegradable litters are not available everywhere so you may need to buy them online.

Creating a happy home

Cats are known for their self-sufficiency, but there are a few items that will help them lead happy, secure lives. These include scratching posts, perches, hide-outs and cat trees, which are especially important if your cat is kept indoors.

BEDS AND BEDDING

Cats will curl up and sleep anywhere, but they like to have a bed of their own. There are various cat beds available. As with most things feline-related, individual cats will have different preferences.

One option is a fake-sheepskin hammock that you hang over a radiator. It provides a cosy spot in winter and cats like the additional security of being up high. A basket lined with a blanket or cushion also makes a cosy space (make sure you choose bedding that is easy to clean).

Bean-bag beds are comfortable and warm, and most cats like them. You can also get hooded 'igloos' made from soft fabric, which offer a private spot. Choose one with a removable cover and wash it regularly.

PERCHES AND HIDE-OUTS

Cats like to get up high. Provide your cat with perches at various points in the home, including at least one that allows it to look out of a sunny window. You can buy window perches to mount on a sill, or you can place a

piece of furniture under the window to create a ready-made window seat. Another good place for a cat perch is on top of a bookcase – the perfect spot for your cat to look down on what is going on in the room.

As well as a high perch, cats like hiding places. They may adopt a spot such as the space under your bed, or may like a cardboard box with a doorway cut out of it.

Below: **A cat igloo is a comfortable, private space that also keeps your cat warm in cold weather because it traps its body heat.**

Above: A cat tree provides your cat with endless entertainment as well as a high perch on which to sleep, or peruse its surroundings.

CAT TREES

A cat tree is an artificial structure designed to keep a cat exercised and entertained. It is an excellent way of providing an indoor cat with places to perch, hide and climb as well as scratch, thus protecting your furniture from damage.

Cat trees come in varying degrees of complexity but will usually feature various climbing stations, scratching posts and a high platform. They are generally made of wood and covered with fabric or carpet and sisal rope. Some also incorporate dens in which the cat can hide (in which case they are known as cat condos). Cat trees are great entertainment, although your cat will also need a selection of toys (see page 122) to keep it amused.

CASE HISTORY
The cats who were shut up

Caroline loved the idea of having cats, and bought two kittens so that they could be company for each other. They grew up to be highly active, and only occasionally sat still and allowed her to pet them. The flat was crammed with ornaments, and Caroline grew tired of the cats knocking them off the shelves, as well as scratching her furniture. So she shut all the doors when she went out in the morning, giving the cats access only to the bathroom and the long hallway.

Eventually, Caroline took in a lodger, Katie, who found the cats intolerable. Rather than lose her flatmate, Caroline decided to rehome the cats and they were collected by a volunteer from a local rescue home. Caroline was shocked when the volunteer told her that the conditions were highly unsuitable for her cats – and that their behaviour was a direct consequence of her inadequate provision for them. She had never considered what kind of an environment a cat might like to live in, and had made her cats highly stressed and unhappy. She decided not to own cats again.

All about carriers

A carrier is essential for transporting your cat, when it is time to go to the veterinarian or on other journeys. Cats don't like to be confined, but a good carrier can make the experience easier and less stressful for you and your cat.

All cats need a carrier. It is not safe to transport them in a car without one because they may become agitated and so constitute a hazard both to themselves and to the driver. Cats generally do not like travelling, but it will help if you can get your cat used to its carrier and making short journeys early on.

A carrier can also be a useful tool in helping your cat to get settled in your home (see page 77), so it is worth buying a good one straightaway. Although temporary cardboard carriers are available, they cannot be cleaned and don't last long.

Right: **There are several different typs of carrier to choose from. A wicker carrier gives the cat privacy and enables it to see out, but can be difficult to clean.**

Above: **Place an old towel or piece of newspaper in the bottom of the carrier in case your cat has an accident when travelling, and take a spare liner with you.**

GETTING YOUR CAT INTO A CARRIER

Make sure that all doors and windows to the room are shut before you pick up your cat – otherwise it is likely to make an escape. Always line your carrier with folded newspaper or an old towel in case of accidents (which usually occur when cats travel), and take a spare lining for the return journey.

Place the carrier on its end on the floor so that the entrance is facing the ceiling. Pick up the cat and take to the carrier. Be firm, but gentle, and be prepared for your cat to struggle when it sees the carrier. Lift into the carrier, tail first. Hold onto the cat until it is safely inside, then quickly close the door and secure it. Slowly move the carrier into the upright position.

Keep your cat in the carrier for the duration of the trip; once you get a cat out of a carrier, it may prove impossible to get it back in. Most cats

CHECKLIST
Carriers

There are various types of carrier to choose from. Some are large enough to house two cats, but you should use these only if you have a pair that gets on very well.

- **All-wire** Made from plastic-covered wire, this type is easy to clean, well-ventilated and secure. You can drape an old towel over the top and back to give your cat privacy.
- **Wicker carrier** This type of carrier allows the cat to see out, while affording it a good degree of privacy. However, it can be hard to clean if your cat has an accident.
- **Plastic carrier** Made from tough plastic, this carrier has solid sides that are vented, with a grid of stainless steel across the door. It is the most practical type of carrier since it is both easy to clean and allows the cat privacy.

will settle down after a time. If your cat is sick when travelling, talk to your veterinarian about the advisability of using tranquillizers.

Do not leave your cat unattended in a car if the weather is hot; the temperature in a car can rise rapidly and cats are susceptible to heatstroke, which can be fatal.

Cat identification

Ensuring your cat is identifiable is an important part of responsible ownership, and the best way of ensuring that it is returned to you if it gets lost. Cat collars and microchipping are effective forms of identification.

Thousands of cats go missing each year, and only a small percentage of these are reunited with their owners. If you allow your cat access to the outdoors, it is vital that it carries adequate identification, so that the finder can contact you in the event it goes astray. An indoor cat is much less likely to go missing, but it may escape if a door or window is inadvertently left open, or it may

Right: **Make sure that you have some good photographs of your cat. If it does go missing, you can make posters or leaflets to show around the neighbourhood.**

even be stolen. In short, all cats need to be easily identifiable.

Remember that neutering your indoor-outdoor cat will reduce the area that it roams, and with it, the risk of it getting lost. You should also keep it indoors at night – from dusk to dawn – which is when most road accidents happen.

COLLARS

A cat collar with a tag is a simple, inexpensive form of identification. Your contact number or address can be engraved onto a disc or written on a piece of paper and placed inside a holder, which can then be attached to the collar. If there is space, include a friend or relative's number, so that the finder will be able to get hold of somebody if you are not available.

Make sure that you use a proper cat collar, rather than one designed for a dog. A cat collar will have an elasticated section or some other means of giving way, to allow the cat to escape if the collar gets caught. This important safety feature does, however, mean that your cat may lose or wriggle out of its collar from time to time. It's a good argument for having your cat microchipped.

When fitting your cat's collar, leave enough space so that you can slip two fingers between the collar and the cat's neck. Check the fit regularly to make sure there is no chafing or skin reaction. If you have a kitten, you should check its collar every few days to make sure it hasn't outgrown it.

MICROCHIPPING

This is the most effective way of ensuring that your cat is identifiable. Microchipping can be carried out by your veterinarian or by an animal charity – it is not expensive, and cat rescue societies may do it at cost price. The procedure is quick and no more painful than an injection. A syringe is used to implant a microchip – the size of a grain of rice – just under your cat's skin between the shoulder blades. The cat is not aware of the microchip once it has been implanted.

The microchip has a unique identification code that can be read by a scanner. This code is held on a database together with your name and contact details, and can also be distributed to rescue centres and veterinarians. Once you have registered with a service, make sure that your contact details are kept up to date.

Although microchipping is a failsafe way to identify your cat, not everybody knows about it. To give your cat the best chance of being returned to you, even if it has been microchipped, you should ensure that it wears a collar too.

Feeding your cat

Cats have unique nutritional needs and require high levels of protein and fat. It's essential to feed your cat the correct diet in order to keep it healthy. Only give supplements on your veterinarian's recommendation – to a pregnant cat, for example.

Cats are what is known as 'obligate carnivores': they need meat and similar foods such as fish in order to survive. They require a large amount of protein relative to their size – more than humans or dogs – as well as a high level of fat. People who do not eat fish or meat themselves may wish to feed their cat a vegetarian diet. However, cats cannot convert vegetable protein and fat into all the nutrients they need. For example, cats need an amino acid called taurine, which they get only from eating meat. (A lack of taurine leads to heart disease and blindness.) Similarly, cats get vitamin A – which is necessary for eye health – from animal sources such as liver and fish oil. So, you cannot feed a cat a vegetarian diet and expect it to stay healthy.

WHAT TO FEED YOUR CAT

In all, your cat requires more than 60 different dietary elements to keep its body functioning well, and these elements need to be given in the right quantities to prevent a deficiency or excess of a particular nutrient. For this reason, it is usually easier to feed your cat a commercial cat food rather than a diet of entirely homemade food. Make sure you choose a reputable, well-known brand – the quality of cat food can

Left: Canned kitten food supplies your kitten with the nutrients it needs for optimum growth. Young cats may also enjoy dried food that has been specially formulated for kittens.

vary considerably. Do not feed dog food to your cat (or vice versa).

A cat's nutritional requirements vary depending on its stage of life. Kittens need more protein than adult cats, while older cats need more vitamins and minerals, and also more easily digestible sources of protein. For these reasons, kittens and older cats should be provided with specially formulated cat foods.

So long as your cat is getting a balanced diet appropriate to its age, it should not need supplements. Giving your cat too much of a particular vitamin or mineral can be harmful. Cats with special dietary requirements should be fed according to the advice of a veterinarian.

Above: **A wild cat gets its nutrients from prey. It buries remains to prevent predators picking up on the scent.**

CHECKLIST
A cat's dietary requirements

A cat needs the following elements in its diet:

- **Protein** All forms of meat and fish provide protein, which should make up at least a quarter of an adult cat's intake, half of a kitten's.
- **Fats** Fat is an essential component of a cat's diet, and should make up around ten per cent of its diet.
- **Carbohydrate** Cats can derive all of their energy needs from meat, so they don't need carbohydrate. However, it is a useful way of bulking up their food, and cats do not seem to have a problem digesting it. It should make up no more than 40 per cent of their diet.
- **Vitamins** An excess or deficiency of a particular vitamin, such as vitamin A, can cause serious problems. However, a balanced diet of mainly commercial cat food should provide all the vitamins a cat needs.
- **Minerals** The most important mineral is calcium, which is needed for healthy bones and teeth. Many other minerals – known as trace minerals – are needed in small amounts. Feeding your cat a good commercial cat food will ensure that it gets the right amount of both major and trace minerals.

COMMERCIAL CAT FOODS

There are two main types of cat food: moist and dry. Most cats like a mixture of both moist and dry foods.

Moist food

Moist food is canned or pouched. It comes in a wide variety of flavours, and has a high water content. Cats generally love moist food. However, it is the most expensive type of cat food and it doesn't keep well. Keep untouched leftovers in the refrigerator, and discard what your cat leaves in the bowl.

Dry food

Dry food does not contain much water, and comes in a bag or box. It is less expensive than other types, and can be left out for your cat to eat when it likes, so long as the cat is not overweight. Dry food gives your cat something to crunch on, which exercises the teeth and gums and helps to keep the teeth tartar-free.

HOMEMADE FOOD AND TREATS

Cats enjoy variety in their food, and so appreciate occasional homemade meals. Favourite foods include cooked meat, chopped into small pieces and served with small amounts of cooked vegetables or pasta to make the meal go further. Chopped cooked chicken or fish (bones removed), or canned fish (bones removed) also go down well, and many cats like lightly scrambled egg, too.

Chocolate is not suitable for cats since it can make them ill. If you want to give your cat treats, choose suitable snacks such as dehydrated prawns or specially formulated cat treats (available from pet shops).

Below: **Dry food is the cheapest form of cat food and helps keep the teeth free of tartar.**

BASIC INSTINCT
Why cats eat grass

Although cats are carnivores, most of them enjoy chewing grass. One theory is that they do this to obtain folic acid. Another is that they eat grass to make themselves vomit, to remove a hairball or other unwanted matter. It's also possible that they do it just because it is enjoyable. If your cat is kept indoors, you should provide it with a tray of suitable grass so that it doesn't have to resort to your houseplants (which may be poisonous).

WATER AND MILK

Cats get most of the water they need from their food, and can therefore drink very little. However, they still need constant access to clean water. Some cats do not like hard water, and may drink more if you filter it first. Others prefer to drink running water from a tap, or even to drink from a puddle or pond. Cats need to drink more water if they are fed dry food; always check with your veterinarian before giving a dry-food-only diet. If you notice that your cat is drinking much more or less than usual, seek advice from your veterinarian.

Kittens need to drink their mother's milk because it has the fat

Above: **If your cat enjoys milk, an occasional bowl shouldn't do any harm. Choose a special 'cat's milk' if your cat reacts badly to cow's milk.**

and protein they need for survival and rapid growth. However, contrary to popular opinion, cats do not need cow's milk. In fact, as they age many cats become lactose-intolerant. They lose the enzyme lactase that enables them to digest lactose, a sugar found in milk, and may get diarrhoea after drinking it. If your cat likes milk and does not react adversely to it, then it is fine to offer it as an occasional treat. You can find 'cat milk' – lactose-free milk suitable for lactose-intolerant cats – in most supermarkets.

Left: **Your cat's food bowl should be shallow enough for it to get at its food without its sensitive whiskers bending.**

HOW MUCH TO FEED

Cats prefer to eat little and often, and will generally eat enough to satisfy their energy requirements and no more. However, if you keep offering your cat more than it needs, it may overeat and become overweight, which will affect its health.

Healthy adult cats should have two meals a day. Offer the daily amount recommended by the manufacturer, and do not give too many snacks between meals.

Cats tend to eat more in winter than in summer, outdoor cats tend to need more food than indoor cats, and older cats eat less than young ones. From day to day, though, a cat's appetite is fairly constant. If your cat stops eating or reduces its intake of food, consult your veterinarian.

Kittens need more frequent meals than adults. This is because they need a high-calorie diet for optimum growth but their small stomachs cannot handle large quantities of food in one go. At 12 weeks, a kitten needs three to four meals a day, reducing to three by six months and two by one year.

All cats like routine, so try to give them their meals at the same time each day.

GENERAL FEEDING GUIDELINES

It's not just what you feed your cat, how you feed it is also important. Cats have a refined sense of smell and taste, and will reject food that is not fresh. They may also turn up their noses if the food is served straight from the refrigerator; cats like their food at room temperature (the temperature, in other words, of freshly killed prey). As cats cannot chew well, they need their food to be chopped into small chunks.

Cats like a calm environment in which to eat, so place their feeding stations in a quieter corner of the kitchen. If you have a dog, then place your cat's food up high where the dog cannot reach it. Do not disturb your cat while it is eating. If you have more than one cat, they will probably prefer separate dishes. For households with many cats, separate feeding places are also often advisable.

Keep your cat's food and water bowl clean – wash after each meal with warm soapy water and rinse well (your cat's sensitive nose may detect any vestiges of a detergent and it will reject its food). A cat's dishes should be shallow and wide, so that it can get at its food and water easily without bending its whiskers. Choose a dish made of a material that does not scratch, like tough plastic or stainless steel.

CHECKLIST
Feeding equipment

- Food bowl
- Water bowl
- Can opener
- Cutlery for serving food
- Plastic box in which to keep cutlery
- Plastic lids to cover half-used cans of cat food
- Automatic feeder, for use if you are away overnight (optional)

Below: **If you have more than one cat they may prefer to eat out of separate dishes. Put your cat bowls in a quiet area of the kitchen.**

Handling your cat

The way that you handle your cat will affect its behaviour and its relationship with you. The most important thing is that your cat feels safe while you are holding it. Supervise young children when they handle a new kitten to make sure it doesn't get hurt.

Always handle your cat confidently, but gently. Any sudden or rough movements will make your cat feel insecure and it may scratch or bite in its attempts to get away. Loud voices also make cats nervous, so try to speak in a quiet, soft tone. It is best to pick up a cat when it is standing, and you are beside it.

PICKING UP A KITTEN OR CAT

To pick up a cat, place one hand just behind its front legs, keeping your index finger between them. Scoop it up, putting the other hand beneath its hindquarters.

Place the hindquarters in the crook of your arm, keeping the cat close to you. Keep your other hand under its chest or over its back, for support. Allow the cat to find a position that it finds comfortable, and don't hold it too tightly. When you want to put the cat down, bend down and place it gently on the floor.

Left: This cat is arching away from the child holding it, a clear signal that it wishes to be put down. Don't hold on to a struggling cat.

Above: **A mother picks up her kittens by the scruff of the neck, but you may damage a fully-grown cat if you try to pick it up like this without supporting the body.**

CHILDREN AND CATS

Children usually try to pick up a cat by grasping it round the abdomen. With young children (under the age of about six), it is best if you hold the cat while they stroke it. Older children can be shown the correct way to hold a cat. Make sure that any children around your cat understand that it must be treated with respect and care. Discourage them from picking it up too often, and from holding the cat if it wants to get down. Keep an especially close eye on your children's contact with a new kitten. A kitten won't be able to get away easily and is susceptible to injury if handled roughly.

STROKING

Most cats like to be stroked, particularly along the neck and back. Stroke in the direction that the fur is growing because a cat does not like to have its fur ruffled. Cats also enjoy having their ears and chest rubbed. The abdomen, though, is a vulnerable area and most cats do not like to be stroked here.

CASE HISTORY
Petting and biting syndrome

Peter's cat Blackthorn enjoys being stroked – most of the time. Occasionally, he will turn on Peter and nip his hand, hard. Once or twice, he has grabbed Peter's wrist with his claws and kicked him with his back legs.

There are two theories behind 'petting and biting syndrome' as it is known. One is that the cat is enjoying the stroking, and relaxes into sleep. It then wakes with a start, realizes it is being confined and instinctively lashes out before escaping. Another possibility is that the stroking has gone on too long. If so, the cat has probably signalled its discomfort by becoming restless, twitching its tail or flattening the ears – signs that Peter should learn to notice. Alternatively, it is possible Peter has transgressed by touching the sensitive belly, which he should avoid in future.

Grooming your cat

Cats generally keep themselves very clean, but all cats benefit from regular grooming sessions from their owners. Get everything ready beforehand – no cat is going to sit patiently while you go off in search of your grooming tools.

How much you groom your cat will depend on how well it can look after its fur when left to its own devices. If it has long hair prone to tangling, you will need to groom it often, while a weekly grooming session is all that's necessary for self-sufficient shorthairs. Grooming reduces the amount of shed hair that ends up on your soft furnishings, and reduces the risk of fur balls in a longhair. It also offers a good opportunity to check the condition of your cat's skin, anal region, ears, eyes, nails and teeth. Grooming your cat regularly makes it

CHECKLIST
Grooming equipment

- Brush and comb, suitable for the length of your cat's fur.
- Adult soft toothbrush, for grooming the face of longhairs.
- Talcum powder, to remove tangles from long coats.
- Spray mister, for longhaired cats.
- Cotton wool, to clean eyes.
- Guillotine-type nail trimmers (available from pet stores).
- Child's soft toothbrush, or special cat toothbrush, to clean teeth.

Left: Grooming is a way of spending time with your cat and enjoying close physical contact. It can help build the bond between owner and pet.

ALLERGIC TO THE CAT?

Allergy sufferers react to cat saliva, which is deposited on the fur, and becomes part of the dander (skin flakes and secretions) that a cat shakes off. Keeping your cat well groomed and bathing it regularly will reduce the amount of dander it produces. Make sure that whoever does the cat grooming doesn't have an allergy – ask a friend, if necessary.

An adult allergy-sufferer with mild symptoms may be able to tolerate a cat in the home, but the bedroom should be a totally cat-free zone, and carpets and soft furnishings need to be kept well cleaned. It will help if the cat bedding is washed regularly (again, by someone without an allergy), if the allergy sufferer avoids the litter tray, and does what they can to limit exposure to any other allergens.

more likely that you will spot any signs of fleas, or any unusual odours, lumps or other abnormalities, which may indicate medical problems.

Grooming your cat also has a psychological purpose: done well, it is an excellent way of promoting a close and trusting bond between owner and cat. Always be gentle and reassuring when grooming.

WHEN TO GROOM

Shorthaired cats need grooming no more than once a week or so. Most longhaired cats, such as Persians, need daily combing. Start grooming your cat young so that it gets used to the process. Keep sessions short and stop when you see signs of agitation such as a twitching tail. Build up the length of the sessions gradually.

Left: **If you have a kitten, groom it regularly. This will help it get used to being handled.**

CLAW CLIPPING

Cats keep their nails trimmed naturally by biting them and by scratching. If their nails get too long, they can get caught in soft furnishings and carpets. The claws may occasionally curl round the pad and dig into it.

Check your cat's claws once a week to ensure they are clean and white. Press the top of the foot and the pads to make the cat fully extend its claws. Remove any debris. If necessary, clip off the sharp tips with a pair of guillotine-type cat trimmers. Cut about two milimetres (0.8 in)

Below: **Check your cat's nails regularly. Active outdoor cats can usually take care of their own nails, but indoor or elderly cats may need their claws clipped once a week or so.**

away from the 'quick', the pink part, which is where the blood supply starts (don't cut this or it will bleed). Indoor cats may need their front claws done once a week (back claws rarely need clipping), while outdoor cats may manage their own claws. Ask your veterinarian for advice if you are unsure. After clipping, give your cat praise and a treat.

GROOMING YOUR CAT'S FUR

You can groom on your lap, or you can place the cat on a table that is a comfortable height. Put down a bath mat to prevent your cat slipping or scratching the table.

Shorthaired cats need a quick brush or comb once a week to remove debris and dead hairs. First, comb through the fur using a fine-toothed comb. Then use a slicker, bristle or rubber brush to brush the coat in the direction it grows. You can also use a grooming glove to do this. For some cats, firm stroking with a hand is all that's needed to keep the coat in good condition.

For a longhaired cat, you'll need a wide-toothed comb and a pin brush. First, comb the hair, section by section, working upwards to remove dead hairs. If you find a knot, work plenty of talcum powder or cornflour into it, and gently tease out by hand. Then brush the fur in sections, working first opposite the direction of growth, then following it. It can help to use a spray bottle to mist the fur with water: this reduces static. Use a soft toothbrush to groom the facial area, then part the tail and brush downwards on either side.

Above: **Choose a time to groom when your cat is in a good mood – don't rouse it from a peaceful slumber because you are ready to groom.**

If your cat's fur becomes very matted, take it to a professional groomer or a veterinarian. It may need to be professionally shaved.

CLEANING THE EYES AND NOSE

After grooming, look at your cat's eyes to check that they are clear of mucus and debris. Longhaired breeds need their eyes cleaning each day as mucus tends to collect in the corners and the tear ducts may become blocked. To remove mucus, moisten a piece of cotton wool with lukewarm water and gently wipe it away (use clean cotton wool for each eye). Clean around the nostrils and nasal folds in the same way.

CHECKLIST
Glossary of brushes

- A **SLICKER BRUSH** has thin, bent tines which help trap loose hair and dirt.
- A **PIN BRUSH** has widely spaced bristles, and is suitable for longhaired cats.
- A **BRISTLE BRUSH** can have hard or soft bristles; soft bristles are good for Oriental-type cats with short, sleek coats, while hard bristles are good for preventing knots in shorthairs with dense fur.
- A **RUBBER BRUSH** is a useful alternative for shorthaired cats that don't like bristle brushes.

CHECKING THE EARS

Check your cat's ears after grooming to make sure they are clean. This helps prevent ear infections and should be a regular part of any grooming routine Remove any excess wax by carefully wiping away with damp cotton wool (or using a proprietary product as recommended by your veterinarian). Do not use a cottonbud, unless directed to do so by your veterinarian – if your cat moves or you push it in too far, you could damage the delicate inside of an ear. Dirt in the ears is a sign of ear mites (see page 165).

Below: **Brushing your cat's teeth and gums regularly will help keep them healthy. Your toothpaste is unsuitable; get your cat a special paste from the pet shop.**

CLEANING THE TEETH

Check your cat's teeth and gums regularly. The teeth should be white, and the gums a healthy pink. A cat's teeth need cleaning two or three times a week to prevent the build-up of tartar, which leads to tooth decay and gum disease. Use a special cat toothbrush and feline toothpaste.

Get your cat used to teeth cleaning as a kitten. Start by simply placing the toothbrush in the mouth, and then gradually progress to cleaning, using plenty of treats to encourage your cat to accept the process. Make sure you clean the back teeth and brush the gums.

BATHING

Cats generally keep themselves very clean, but if your cat's fur is especially soiled you may need to give it a bath. Few cats enjoy being wet, making bathing tricky to manage. It will be easier on both of you if you handle your cat confidently and firmly – and if you have an assistant. Use special cat shampoo as recommended by your veterinarian. If your cat will let you, place cotton-wool balls in its ears to keep them dry (remember to remove them afterwards).

First, brush your cat thoroughly to remove any tangles. Place a small folded towel in the base of the sink or an old baby bath to make a non-slip surface. Fill to a depth of one quarter with just-warm water. Manoeuvre your cat into the sink or bath – hold it by the scruff of the neck to keep it still, but support its hindquarters.

Use a jug to pour water over your cat. Then apply the shampoo, making sure none gets into your cat's eyes, ears or mouth. Do the neck and back first, then tail and bottom, then the legs and feet, before finishing with the face and head (it can be easier to use a facecloth to do this part). Lather it all over, then rinse off with clean water. You will have to change

the water your cat is standing in a few times. Apply separate conditioner, if using, and rinse well.

Wrap your cat in a large towel, and gently dry the fur (some cats will tolerate gentle blow-drying on a low heat). Keep the cat in a warm room until the fur is completely dry – cats can easily become chilled.

Below: Few cats like to be bathed, but they can learn to tolerate it if you start when they are young. Some cats will even allow you to shower their fur rather than using a jug.

Holiday care

There are bound to be times when you need to be away from home. Ensuring that your cat is well looked after in your absence will minimize its distress but be aware that any professional care may be costly.

Cats should not be left alone for long, so if you are going to be away for more than 24 hours, you will need to arrange care. Many cats prefer to stay at home with someone feeding them twice a day. You may be able to get a neighbour, relative or friend to do this for you – or you can pay a pet-sitting service. Cats can get lonely if left alone for long periods, so having a familiar person to stay in your home is usually the best option.

Some people take their cat away with them, or send the cat to another home to be cared for. Since cats are territorial, they naturally find it unsettling to be taken away from their normal surroundings. If you need to do this, taking some familiar items, such as the cat's bedding, will help it cope better. Ideally, create a 'safe room' (see page 77) wherever your cat goes.

CATTERIES

Taking your cat to a boarding cattery is another holiday care option to consider. Your veterinarian may be able to recommend one. Otherwise, ask cat-owning friends and relatives in your area. Your cat will need to have its vaccinations up to date (and most catteries will not take animals suffering from contagious diseases, such as FeLV).

Always look round a prospective cattery, and talk to the proprietor or manager. Ideally, each cat should be allocated its own purpose-built accommodation with an enclosed sleeping area, resting platform and an outdoor run. There should be good ventilation between runs to prevent airborne diseases from spreading.

YOUR CAT'S DETAILS

When you arrange cat care, don't forget to leave details about your cat's feeding and litter-cleaning schedule with the carer, together with information about any medication your cat is receiving. You should also leave your contact number in case of emergency, together with a number for your veterinarian and your cat's insurance details.

CHECKLIST
Cat care options

CATTERY
Pros
- Simple to arrange
- Safe and secure
- Carers understand cats

Cons
- Costly
- Vaccinations must be up to date
- Catteries don't accept cats that are ill or have infectious diseases

PET SITTER
Pros
- Cat has company
- Cat will be looked after by person who likes animals
- Your home will also be looked after

Cons
- May be costly
- Often involves having a stranger in your home

STAYING WITH CARER
Pros
- Free
- Cat will have company

Cons
- Unsettling for cat
- Cat may get lost if it goes outdoors

VISITING CARE AT HOME
Pros
- Free
- Cat remains in its own environment

Cons
- Cat left alone most of the time
- Carer may not see the cat when visiting to leave food
- If cat has an accident or becomes ill, it may not get help quickly

Each cat should have its own scratching post and plenty of toys. You should be allowed to send familiar bedding or toys with your cat to help it feel more settled. Make sure you book early because a good cattery will be quickly filled during peak periods.

Right: **If your cat has to go away from home, make sure it has familiar items such as its bed, bedding and a favourite toy to help it settle.**

Moving home

Moving is an upheaval for all the family, including your cat. You need to plan carefully to minimize your cat's anxiety and prevent it from getting lost before or after the move. Don't let it roam freely until it is accustomed to its new home.

Cats become very attached to their surroundings, and moving is stressful for them. You need to make sure that they are taken care of on the day. It may be best to keep the cat out of the way entirely by booking it into a cattery for a few days.

PREPARING TO MOVE

If you want to keep your cat with you, designate a 'safe room' at your old home. Clear this out a week or so before the move and place your cat's bed, litter tray, scratching post and so on here. If possible, feed your cat here so it gets used to the space. Put your cat in the room the evening before the move, and keep it there while all the loading is done.

When you are ready to leave, place your cat in the carrier and take it to the new abode. Designate a 'safe room' here, and keep your cat in this room for several days (as when you first settled it into your family; see page 77). When you let it out, remember to keep all doors, windows and cat flaps closed while your cat explores its new home.

Left: **Transport your cat in its carrier and take it straight to a safe room so it can get used to its new home gradually.**

If you have an indoor-outdoor cat, don't let it out until it is thoroughly at home (the minimum recommended time is two weeks). When you do let it out, do so just before a mealtime. Go out with your cat and leave the door open so it can run back into the home. Let it out for short periods only, until you judge the time ready to give it more freedom. Don't forget to update your address on your microchip registry.

Right: **After a few days in the same room, your cat should be ready to explore the home. Keep the door open so it can retreat to its safe space.**

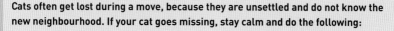

CHECKLIST
Tips for finding a missing cat

Cats often get lost during a move, because they are unsettled and do not know the new neighbourhood. If your cat goes missing, stay calm and do the following:

- Check your home thoroughly, especially likely hiding places such as wardrobes, coal-chutes, cellars and sheds.
- Take a photograph door to door round your neighbourhood. Leave your contact details.
- Go back to your old home. Leave your contact details and a photograph of your cat with the new owners and the neighbours.
- Ring round all the rescue centres in your area to see if your cat has been taken in. Do this every couple of days.
- Make a poster of your cat. Include the words 'Lost Cat' in large type, a

- good-quality photograph and a brief description of your cat, mentioning any identifying marks, plus your mobile and landline numbers.
- Post your cat's details on missing pet websites (enter 'lost pet' into a search engine to find these).
- Look for your cat at night, when it is quiet. Take food with you and a cat carrier.
- Go to the bottom of your garden in the night, and listen; your cat may be trapped somewhere and calling for you.
- Keep a pen and paper by the phone to note down the finder's details.

Games and training

It is sometimes said that cats cannot be trained, but that is a myth. Cats can be taught many things – and they have to learn some basics if your relationship is to be harmonious. This chapter shows you how to get your cat to behave in the way that you want – so long as you, the owner, have reasonable expectations.

If cats don't get what they need, or if they become stressed, they can react in some unappealing ways. This section highlights all the common behavioural problems, explaining the possible causes and suggesting ways to put things right.

Cats love to play, and this is also a great way of making sure that they get the exercise they need. The following pages contain plenty of ideas for games, as well as suggestions for toys that your cat will enjoy – because an active cat is invariably a happy cat.

Play and the cat

Cats love to play as kittens, and continue to enjoy games right through to old age. Regular playtime is a great way of making sure an indoor cat gets enough exercise to keep it healthy and prevent stress or boredom.

Cats, as natural hunters, are built for exercise. Domestic cats, of course, have no need to hunt for their food, so they may not get the exercise they need to stay fit and healthy.

Cats vary in the amount of exercise they do. Outdoor cats get plenty of opportunities to prowl and hunt, and usually self-regulate their need for activity. Indoor cats rely on their owners to provide them both with an environment that encourages activity and also with plenty of play opportunities.

Some breeds of cat are naturally more active than others – the Abyssinian and the Siamese, for example, are known for their

get-up-and-go. Individual cats may have differing requirements for exercise. If your cat seems very inactive or is overweight, seek advice from your veterinarian. Similarly, if a normally active cat loses interest in play, your veterinarian is the best person to consult.

Below: **Play does much more than keep kittens amused. It is how they learn their place in the litter, how to fight, and – just as importantly – when to back off.**

- Let your cat set the agenda. If it doesn't want to play right now, don't try to force it.
- Let your cat win most of the time, but make it work for its victory.
- Put most toys out of sight after use. That way, your cat will be interested when you get them out again.
- Always have a rotating selection of toys available so your cat can keep itself amused.
- Play often. A couple of 15-minute sessions a day is ideal.

- Be regular: cats appreciate routine, so schedule set times for play.
- Be prepared to stop the session when your cat gets tired, loses interest or becomes agitated.
- Don't bring a game to a sudden stop. It's much better to calm an activity down gradually.
- Don't use your hands or feet as part of the game – it may be fun to let a kitten pounce on them, but its claws and teeth will get a lot sharper as it gets older.

WHAT PLAY DOES

Play has lots of benefits. It helps your cat maintain a good weight, keeps the joints supple, and helps the heart and lungs stay healthy. Play also keeps a cat occupied and prevents boredom or stress. It provides a harmless outlet for the cat's natural hunting instincts, and it helps a cat to release aggressive or nervous energy. Above all, playing with your cat is fun for you both, and can help to strengthen the relationship between you.

Cats start to play in the litter. This is how they learn essential life skills, such as fighting, restraint and hunting. At first they play with their siblings, then – at about eight weeks – they become interested in inanimate objects. They start to practise chasing, pouncing and batting – all the skills they need when it comes to catching live prey.

Above: **An outdoor cat with plenty of space to roam will usually get its exercise through prowling and running.**

Toys and games

There are many games that you can play with your cat, and you should also make sure it has ways to entertain itself when you are not there. You need a variety of games and activities to keep your cat stimulated and occupied.

Cats are usually at their most active early in the morning and late at night, which makes these good times to schedule play. Giving your cat 15 minutes of interactive play in the evening may encourage it to sleep more during the night.

HUNTING GAMES

A cat learns to hunt through playing with its littermates, and hunting games remain its favourite for the rest of its life. There is nothing a cat likes better than to chase a toy that you pull across the floor, or dangle above its head. The 'prey' can be as simple as a piece of string, or you can buy a fishing-rod toy with a feather or bell attached. Some cats adore jumping at a light beam from a laser pointer (use these with caution).

Toys that skid across the floor when batted are a good way to give your cat the thrill of the chase. Small balls – such as ping pong balls – clean wine corks or the plastic top of a large milk container are ideal, and will give your cat many hours of fun. (Always supervise this type of play to make sure nothing is swallowed, and put away small items after use. Corks that are bitten should be discarded.)

Left: **A fishing-rod toy is inexpensive and offers plenty of entertainment. Your cat will adore playing with it, and the toy will keep your hands well away from its sharp teeth and claws.**

Wind-up toys can be set off to go in various directions – a simple clockwork one is great, or you can get remote-controlled toys that are designed especially for cats. Set a toy mouse on course for a cardboard box with a large doorway cut out of it. If your cat doesn't catch the mouse before it's inside, it will have to tease it out with its paw.

FIND THE TREAT

Another variant of the hunting game is to hide dried cat food or treats, and leave your cat to find them. Get a selection of boxes and paper bags, and place a few treats inside. Make it harder for your cat to get them by partially closing boxes or, say, placing a treat under some scrunched-up paper in an egg box or inside a crumpled piece of paper in an empty toilet-roll tube. Make sure the containers are cat-safe – cut handles off paper bags, and check for staples. You can glue several boxes together and cut holes in them for added fun.

Right: **A wind-up toy is a good way to keep your cat occupied. Check for damage before each playtime.**

An even simpler version of this game is to hide some cat treats in different places around the room. If your cat has trouble finding them, drag a treat across the floor to leave a scent trail when it is not looking.

BASIC INSTINCT **Stalking practice**

Play teaches cats hunting and stalking manouvres that are essential survival skills. Remember that in the wild your cat would stalk its prey through the undergrowth. You can replicate this experience to a degree by draping a towel from a kitchen chair, then dangling the prey so that your cat goes through the den. Or try placing a newspaper or a cloth on the floor and dragging a toy underneath it.

NOISY TOYS

Cats love interesting noises and will happily play for long periods with, for example, crinkly sweet wrappers or a ball with a bell inside. Newspapers are inherently attractive to felines – try laying your paper on the floor and then pulling it gently when your cat comes to sit on it. Your cat will love the sound made when it pounces on the moving newspaper and tears it to shreds.

CATNIP TOYS

Give your cat a soft toy stuffed with catnip. This is a herb of the mint family that has a euphoric effect on cats. Catnip can also trigger frenzied behaviour – such as rolling and leaping about – or it can induce a trancelike state. Whatever the effect, it is short-term, lasting ten minutes or so, and seems to cause no harm.

Above: **A cat DVD will keep a cat amused, helping to fend off boredom, particularly if it features other animals and sounds of wildlife.**

You can grow your own catnip, dry it and use the leaves to stuff a simple soft toy, or you can buy ready-made catnip toys from pet shops. You can also let your pet chew on the leaves of the plant. (Grow catnip in containers rather than in a flowerbed. Like all mints, catnip is invasive and can quickly grow out of control.)

OTHER EXERCISE FOR INDOOR CATS

Cats like playing with each other, as well as with their human companions. If you have an indoor cat, consider getting another so that they can enjoy chasing each other around the home (see page 52).

All cats love play equipment such as cat trees. If your cat is kept indoors, this is essential kit both to keep it active and to provide a natural outlet for natural behaviours such as climbing. Leave a variety of toys out for your cat to play with, but make sure they are in good condition and safe for it to use unsupervised.

WALKING ON A LEASH

Some indoor cats can be trained to walk on a leash. This can be a great way of giving them exercise and introducing them safely to the outside world. Always walk with your cat during a quiet time of day, such as early in the morning when there are not too many people about. Don't expect your cat to follow you obediently like a dog. Your cat will want to lead the way.

CHECKLIST
Toy safety

- Never leave your cat alone to play with pieces of string, cord or similar.
- Throw away broken toys with sharp edges, or worn soft toys if the filling is in danger of coming out.
- Make sure all soft toys are washable and keep them clean.
- Don't leave plastic carrier bags around, because cats like to get into them.
- Cut the handles off paper bags and remove any staples.
- Always ensure any toys you give your cat are non-toxic.
- Don't let your cat play with rubber bands, tinsel, deflated balloons or small objects such as paperclips, which could be swallowed.

Right: **Most cats love playing with catnip toys. If the toy is a few weeks old, put it in the microwave for a few seconds to refresh the catnip scent.**

Setting the rules

It's often said that cats are hard to train. But cats are clever creatures. They can easily learn the rules of the house, provided that you are consistent in what you ask. Training is most effective when you reward rather than punish your cat.

Your cat's natural curiosity and instinctive ability to learn makes it eminently trainable – especially when it is young. The earlier you start training, the more successful you are likely to be. The first rule is consistency. Decide what the basic rules of the house are, and stick to them. For example, if you do not want your cat to fuss around you

when you are eating dinner, do not feed it from your plate as a special treat. Cats need clear guidelines, and it is important that all members of the family stick to them.

If you are training your cat to do something specific – such as walk on a leash – keep training sessions short and simple. It will respond best if you train every day, when it is hungry. Bear in mind that a cat will not learn if it is bored or confused.

POSITIVE REINFORCEMENT

Cats learn by trial and error, observation, imitation and when it is in their interests to learn how to perform a task. When teaching a cat to act in a certain way it's best to give it plenty of praise and to reward it with a tasty treat, such as a dehydrated prawn, when it has completed the task. Once the cat has learned the behaviour, give the treat intermittently rather than every time to reinforce the behaviour.

Left: **Teach your cat to recognize its name by using it regularly, especially when you feed and stroke it.**

BASIC INSTINCT **How cats learn**

Many people say that cats are less intelligent than dogs because they can do fewer tricks. However, dogs live in packs in the wild, and are hardwired with a desire to please the pack leader (a role that in the domestic sphere is ascribed to their human owners). Cats are solitary animals, and they need a different incentive to learn. If the task is too difficult, or the prospect of reward uncertain, cats will find something else to do – just as in the wild they would give up and find easier prey.

Cats learn most effectively through positive reinforcement, and swiftly realize that certain types of behaviour result in reward. A domestic cat will work out, for example, that a pitiful miaow will get a compliant owner to hand out a treat. Your cat may teach itself to perform useful feats, such as opening a refrigerator door, by watching how you do it and experimenting with different techniques. This kind of problem-solving ability is undoubtedly a sign of a special feline intelligence.

NEGATIVE REINFORCEMENT

Never strike a cat, no matter how angry you are with its behaviour. It is proven not to help with training, and hitting is likely to make your cat stressed, which can lead to behaviour problems. Many experts recommend using a water pistol to squirt a cat when it engages in undesirable behaviour – such as walking on your kitchen worktops. You should be able to train your cat not to do this simply by removing it every time it jumps up and placing it on the floor with a gentle reprimand. However, if you do need to resort to water squirting, be sure to aim at the cat's rear rather than its face.

Right: **There's no doubt that cats are clever enough to learn tricks, such as opening a door, but they do things for their own benefit rather than to please their owners.**

Litter training

Cats are naturally clean animals. They want their living space to be tidy and dirt-free. Training a cat to use a litter tray is usually straightforward because it chimes with their natural instincts. Give plenty of praise when training and keep the tray clean.

TRAINING A KITTEN

Kittens learn to use a litter tray by copying the mother cat, so your kitten should already be using a tray by the time you bring it home. Your task is simply to reinforce this early training in the new environment.

When you bring your kitten home, keep it in a bathroom or other room that can be easily cleaned. Show the kitten where the litter tray is and place it in it so that it can explore. It may help if you move the litter around with your hand.

Below: **Place your kitten in the litter tray so that it knows where its latrine is. You may want to move its paws to help it scratch.**

CHECKLIST
Litter training tips

- Place the litter tray somewhere that is easily accessible.
- Don't put the litter tray in a busy area of the home. Choose a place that is safe and quiet.
- Keep the litter tray away from food and water bowls.
- In a multi-cat household, put out one litter tray for each cat, plus one extra.
- Put a litter tray on each floor if you have a multi-storey home.
- Make sure the tray is kept clean. Your cat will not use a dirty or smelly tray.
- Use a litter your cat likes (most prefer clumping litters – see page 90).

Cats have a natural instinct not to soil the nest, which would alert predators to their presence and also put them at risk of infection and disease. Very young kittens are unable to eliminate without being stimulated by the mother's licking; this is to ensure that the mother is there to clean up any waste. Once they are mobile, the mother will stimulate their elimination function only when they are outside the nest. This is the kitten's first toileting lesson.

Place your kitten in the litter tray after mealtimes, when it is most likely to move its bowels, and after sleep times, or if you see it sniffing, scratching or crouching in a corner. Don't punish your kitten if it has an accident, but gently place it on the litter tray. Give it lots of praise while it is there. It will help if you use the same type of tray and litter that your kitten was used to before you brought it home, at least at the start.

TRAINING AN ADULT CAT

Adult cats can take a little longer than kittens to use a litter tray if they are not used to it. If you are training a new cat, start off in a safe room. Otherwise simply show your cat where the litter tray is, and encourage it to explore the tray by moving the litter around with your hand. Speak softly and encouragingly if your cat gets onto the litter tray.

Praise your cat if it uses the litter tray, and give it a treat. Give your cat privacy when it is actually using the box – cats do not like to be watched. If your cat misses the tray, pick up the faeces with a scoop and place it in the tray, covering it with some litter. Clean the area thoroughly or your cat is likely to use the spot again. Use a dilute solution of biological detergent or an enzyme-containing product to eliminate all traces of odour.

Never punish your cat by rubbing its nose in the faeces or smacking it. These kinds of punishments simply create fear in the cat, which may well trigger more toileting problems.

Below: **Keep the litter tray in a bathroom or other room that can be easily cleaned. Give your cat a treat after it has used the tray.**

Using a cat flap

A cat flap enables your cat to enter and exit the home without your help. Training your cat to use a flap can take longer than you might expect. But with patience – and a couple of tricks – most cats will use one eventually.

Cat flaps can be great for indoor–outdoor cats, as they allow them free access to the outside world. You can also use flaps to allow an indoor cat access to a screened porch or cat run, or to give your cat access to a room where the litter tray is kept and at the same time keeping your dog out. Some cat flaps come with a locking device, which is useful for keeping your cat in at night.

These benefits are not apparent to your cat, who may at first view the flap with suspicion. Cats cannot be forced to do anything they do not wish to. Training your cat to use the flap is all about creating a positive association with a desired behaviour. The last thing you should do is pick up an unwilling cat and force it through a flap. You may get badly scratched or, worse, your cat may view the flap with aversion and refuse to use it at all.

Left: **Food treats are the most effective way of encouraging a reluctant cat to go through a cat flap. Once your cat gets used to the flap, it will go through it happily without needing a reward.**

STEP-BY-STEP CAT-FLAP TRAINING

Show your cat what lies beyond the cat flap by propping it open. Use string or strong adhesive tape to do this (or remove the flap altogether). Encourage your cat to come through it by placing a food treat on the inside – this is easier than trying to entice it outside.

Once your cat is happy doing this, lure it outside in the same way. Then gradually lower the flap a little each day until your cat learns how to push the door open. Use food treats – ideally something with a strong smell, such as sardines – to encourage your cat to head-butt the door. Take it slowly – many cats take a couple of weeks, some even longer, to get used to a cat flap.

CAT-FLAP TECHNOLOGY

Outdoor cat flaps can give a dominant neighbourhood cat access to your home, which will threaten your cat's security. Other animals aside from cats (such as foxes) have also been known to use them. One solution is to install an electromagnetic cat door, which is operated

Above: **Propping a cat flap open shows your cat that there is nothing lying in wait on the other side. Let your cat take its time – forcing a cat to do something is generally counterproductive.**

by a gadget attached to your cat's collar, to eliminate this possibility. An alternative – which may be more suitable if your cat won't keep a collar on – is a battery-operated cat flap that responds to your cat's microchip (see page 97).

BASIC INSTINCT **Why cats come in and out so often**

Indoor-outdoor cats can drive their owners to distraction by insisting on being let out, then two minutes later demanding to be let back in again. This behaviour may be annoying for you, but the cat is merely patrolling his territory indoors and out, checking for intruders and renewing its scent markers as it goes. The doors of your home (without flaps) are an irrelevant and incomprehensible obstacle to your cat. Irritating as this is for you, it's frustrating for them that they cannot pass through without your help.

Walking on a leash

Some cats can be trained to walk on a leash. Depending on where you live, this can be a good way of giving an otherwise indoor cat experience of the sights and sounds of the outside world. Do not try to direct it – let your cat decide where to go.

The first step towards getting your cat to walk on a leash is to get it used to a harness or a walking jacket (cats should not be leashed with a collar). Go about this slowly. First, leave the harness in a prominent place where your cat can explore it. You can make it smell like your cat by rubbing a cloth over your pet and then rubbing it over the harness.

When your cat is used to seeing the harness, place it over its head for a few seconds only (do not tighten at this stage). Give your cat lots of praise and a treat for accepting this. Do this repeatedly over the following days and weeks, each time rewarding your cat with more praise and food treats. Gradually progress to tightening the harness and leaving it on for a few minutes at a time. If your cat objects at any point, stop and try again later.

Below: **A cat harness should be shaped like an H or a figure of eight, and the leash should attach between the shoulder blades.**

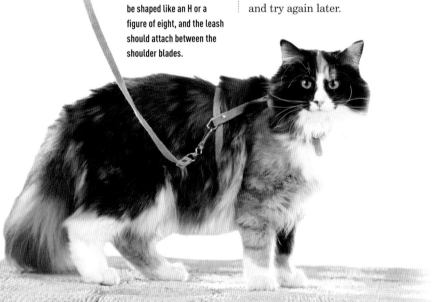

Once your cat is happy wearing the harness, attach the lead to it. Let your cat walk around with the leash attached. When it accepts this, you can pick up the end of the leash and walk your cat around the home. Keep the leash slack and let your cat dictate where you go.

Do make sure the harness is comfortable. You should be able to slip two fingers between the harness

Above: **You can walk your cat round your garden or take it into a quiet area. Avoid places where dogs are walked off the leash.**

and the cat's body. Always loop the leash around your wrist so that you cannot drop it.

MOVING OUTDOORS

The next stage is to go outdoors with your cat. At first stick to your garden or doorstep, then gradually venture further if your area is safe. Go out at quiet times of day – such as early in the morning – and keep outings very short. Don't expect your cat to follow you like a dog. A walk with a cat is much less directed. Let it pause to sniff an interesting odour, lie in the sun or roll in the dust.

If your cat is startled by a dog, it may try to run off. Scooping it up and shielding it from the dog's view may be necessary. Carry a towel or jacket that you can throw around the cat before you pick it up so that you don't get scratched.

Cat-walking tips

As with any form of cat behaviour training, you need to be patient: a cat will not be rushed. It can take several weeks – several months with some animals – to train a cat to walk on a leash. Train just before mealtimes, when your cat is hungry and therefore most receptive, for a few minutes at a time. You will get the best results if you are consistent and train your cat each day, taking it one step at a time.

Why cats misbehave

Cats are usually easy to live with, but when things go wrong, they can go *very* wrong. Establishing the reason for unwanted behaviour is usually the first step towards fixing it and restoring harmony to your household.

It is important to remember that most problem behaviours are not a problem to the cat. Many problem behaviours are actually things that are completely normal when performed in the wild – urine spraying, scratching, and eating plants, for example, are all things that a cat does quite naturally outdoors. Others, such as overgrooming, may be a natural behaviour taken to extreme. Sometimes the solution may be as simple as providing the cat with a more acceptable outlet for its behaviour. You may also need to understand the ways in which a cat behaves and communicates in the wild to come up with a solution.

MEDICAL CAUSES

Symptoms of ill health can be difficult to spot, and a medical problem can manifest itself as a behaviour issue. Seek the advice of a veterinarian if your cat starts to behave in a strange and inexplicable way – for example, by constantly biting at a particular area of the body. Sudden behaviour changes can point to a medical issue. Occasionally, medication, such as anti-anxiety drugs, may be appropriate.

Left: **There's usually a good reason for a cat's actions. If you don't like an aspect of your cat's behaviour, you need to find a way to redirect it.**

ANIMAL BEHAVIOURISTS

Cat owners can be remarkably tolerant about their cat's behaviour. It's not uncommon to hear of a cat relieving itself in, say, a living area for years on end. Once a behaviour has become habitual, it is difficult to eradicate, and you may need to seek advice from a professional animal behaviourist. Animal behaviourists can help you to uncover the cause of a behaviour and develop a suitable treatment plan to improve your cat's behaviour. One appointment may be all that is needed for a simple problem, but most behaviourists offer follow-up phone calls and aftercare. Your veterinarian should be able to refer you to a reputable animal behaviourist.

STRESS AND ANXIETY

Cats can become stressed or anxious if there are unwelcome changes in their environment, and may react by altering their behaviour. If your cat displays a new unwanted behaviour, consider what has been going on in the home. The arrival of a new animal or person (such as a baby), bereavement or stress in the family, decorating or building works can all trigger stress in the cat.

ENVIRONMENT

Indoor cats are much more likely to exhibit problem behaviours because they often lack natural outlets for instinctive behaviours. Looking at the environment you are providing for your cat can be key to understanding its behaviour.

YOUR ROLE

Consider whether your expectations are reasonable. If you feed your cat from your plate, then get annoyed when it miaows when you are eating, you are being inconsistent. Likewise, if you don't want it to scratch your furniture, then it is only fair to provide it with an alternative such as a scratching post.

Left: **Be consistent about what you expect. If you don't want your cat on your worktops, take it off every single time it jumps up.**

Toileting problems

Any form of inappropriate toileting is hard for owners to live with. When it happens, it is essential to work out what lies behind the behaviour so that you can put a stop to it early on and prevent it from becoming a habit.

Toileting problems are miserable for everyone in the household, and are a key reason for cats being admitted to rescue centres. Before you consider solutions, you need to know whether your cat is marking, or relieving itself. Generally speaking, if a cat urinates on a wall or other vertical surface, it is marking its territory; if it urinates on a horizontal surface then it is relieving itself. Deposits of faeces can be either a marker or a sign of a toileting problem.

Below: **When a cat sprays, it backs up to a vertical surface and releases a small amount of strong-smelling urine. It will often return to the same place in order to refresh the scent.**

SPRAYING IN THE HOME

Spraying in the home is unusual, or should be. It can indicate a medical problem, which should be ruled out by a veterinarian. More commonly, though, a cat sprays to mark its territory, often in the areas where it feels unsafe. As the home is a cat's safe base, it should not need to spray here. If it does, it may mean that your cat's sense of territory has been threatened in some way. There are many reasons why this may have happened – the arrival of another cat in the home, decorating work, even a new piece of furniture placed in a favourite spot. Sometimes, all that is needed to trigger spraying is for the cat to catch a glimpse of a rival cat in the garden from a window.

You may be able to work out the cause of your cat's spraying from the

place it is doing it. If it is on a cat flap, then it is possible there is a threat – or perceived threat – from a neighbourhood cat. If you have recently brought a cat into the home, and the spraying is in an internal doorway, this may be where the cats have to pass each other.

PUTTING A STOP TO SPRAYING

Cats like to spray in the same place. To prevent your cat from making a return visit, remove all traces of odour using a dilute solution of biological detergent or an enzyme-containing cleaner. Never use a cleaner that contains ammonia as this is a component of cat urine and will encourage more spraying. Some surfaces can also be sprayed with surgical spirit to remove any last traces of scent (check that the surface won't be damaged by this by doing a patch test first).

Above: **Cats mark out their territory by spraying urine as an olfactory 'keep out' message to other cats. When a cat sprays in the home it is generally a sign that the cat feels threatened.**

Other ways to make an area unappealing are by spraying it with a citrus scent (which cats dislike) or covering the floor with aluminium foil, which your cat won't want to walk on. Placing food in a problem area can also be a way of deterring a cat from spraying. Another option is to use a synthetic pheromone, which mimics the substances produced by a cat when rubbing to mark its territory. These are available in spray form, or you can buy a pheromone diffuser. The scent helps a cat feel safe, which deters spraying.

Keep the cat away while you clean, then supervise its return. If you see your cat back up to the wall with an upright tail, push the tail downwards and distract your cat with a game.

Above: **If stress is behind your cat's toileting problem, give it lots of attention and take steps to remove any challenges you can. Confining your cat to one room for a short period can help calm anxiety.**

TREATING THE CAUSE

If your cat is spraying for stress reasons, take any steps you can to make its environment less challenging. If another cat is getting into the home, fit a magnetic cat flap that can be opened only by your cat. If your cat is bothered by seeing other cats through a window, use semi-transparent film to cover the glass. If two or more cats have to pass by each other in the area, position shelving or furniture to allow them to pass on different

levels. You should also make sure that your cat's environment is suitable and stimulating enough (see pages 92–3).

If the problem persists, it can be helpful to isolate your cat in a safe room for several days, then gradually reintroduce it to the rest of the home (see pages 80–1) once it starts using the litter box correctly. The safe room is a way of removing your cat from a challenging situation and calming any anxiety. Make sure that you provide for all its needs and visit several times a day. Give your cat lots of loving attention and regular playtime to reduce stress.

LITTERING OUTSIDE THE TRAY

There are many reasons why a cat toilets in an inappropriate place. Working out the trigger for your cat's behaviour may be a matter of systematically considering all the possibilities, and dealing with them one by one.

Think about the basics. Cats are very sensitive to any changes to their routine or toileting environment. They may refuse to use a litter tray if it is dirty, if they dislike the type of litter, or if there is not quite enough litter in the box. You can also put your cat off its tray by cleaning it with a scented product or strong-smelling disinfectant.

If you have recently replaced your cat's open tray with a hooded type, it may be deterred from using it because it dislikes being enclosed. Similarly, if you have moved the location of the tray, it may now be in a place that is too busy or does not meet your cat's need to feel safe and private when using its latrine.

If a change has triggered your cat's toileting behaviour, then the simplest way to deal with it is to return to whichever system you were using before. As with a spraying problem, always clean any soiled areas thoroughly to remove any odour and discourage re-use. If your cat is using a particular area as its toilet, discourage it by covering the surface with a material your cat will be reluctant to step on, such as aluminium foil, plastic sheeting or double-sided tape.

MULTI-CAT HOUSEHOLDS

If you have more than one cat, it can be difficult to work out which cat is toileting inappropriately. You may need to seek advice from an animal behaviourist. Make sure that there are sufficient litter trays for the cats – one tray per cat, plus one extra is a good formula – and that they are cleaned out regularly. Providing additional places to sleep, eat, drink, scratch and play can also help your cats to feel secure. Bear in mind that toileting problems can be a sign that a cat is being bullied by another cat (see also pages 142–3).

Below: **When a normally litter-trained cat goes outside the tray, it may be because the tray is dirty, or because there has been a change to the litter-tray environment. If you have more than one cat, make sure there are enough litter trays.**

MEDICAL CAUSES

When your cat experiences toileting problems, you should always consider the possibility that it is ill. Urinary tract or bladder infections are a common reason for cats avoiding the litter tray – if your cat experiences a burning sensation when urinating, it will associate the pain with the litter tray and refuse to use it again. Similarly, a constipated cat will be uncomfortable passing a stool and associate this discomfort with its litter tray.

Your cat may have diarrhoea, worms or be urinating more than usual as a result of a particular illness, such as diabetes, or a medication, such as a steroid. Either of these conditions could make it hard for a cat to reach its litter tray

Above: **If your cat regularly uses an area near an external door as a latrine, it may be sending a keep-away message to other cats or human intruders, such as visitors to your house.**

in time. Alternatively, it may simply be too sick or elderly to get to the litter tray. If there is no immediately obvious cause for your cat avoiding its litter tray, take it to a veterinarian for a thorough check-up. Some illnesses are hard to spot, and your veterinarian may need to conduct blood, urine or stool tests to pinpoint the cause.

STRESS AND ANXIETY

If you cannot find an environmental or physical cause for your cat's toileting behaviour, the cause may be psychological. An unpleasant

Above: **Many illnesses can trigger toileting problems. If there is no obvious cause for your cat's inappropriate toileting, seek advice from a veterinarian.**

experience such as being shouted at when it is relieving itself can lead to a cat avoiding the litter tray afterwards. Changing the litter tray or moving it to a different place can be helpful as it breaks the association with a negative event. It may be necessary to confine the cat to the same room as the tray while you retrain (see also page 77).

Cats use faeces, as well as urine, to mark an area with their scent. This is known as middening. Faeces in the home could be your cat's way of responding to some kind of territorial threat. The threat could be anything from the presence of another cat in the garden to having builders or decorators in the home. As with spraying, to deal with the problem, you first need to remove any traces of odour, and then take steps to help your cat feel more secure (see page 136).

(see also page 77). (see page 136).

CASE HISTORY
The message on the bed

Whenever Gale and John went on holiday, their daughter at home would look after the cat Cleo. The year she moved out, they arranged for a neighbour to pop in and feed Cleo instead. On their return they made a huge fuss of her, but to their horror, the following day they found a neat pile of faeces right in the middle of their bed.

- -

The deposit of faeces on her owners' bed – the place that smelled most of them – was Cleo's way of marking her territory. Middening, as it is known, is evidence of insecurity, triggered in this case by a stranger coming into the home when the owners were absent. The next time Gale and John went away, they arranged for Cleo to go to a cattery. To their relief, there was no repeat of the gift on the bed.

When cats attack

Aggression is natural in cats, but in the domestic situation they have no real need to fight. Nevertheless, their innate aggression may sometimes rise to the surface. Be careful when dealing with an aggressive cat or you may get hurt.

Cats can ambush you by pouncing on your ankles as you walk by. In this case, they are playing rather than trying to hurt you, but their sharp teeth and claws make it an unwelcome game. If your cat does this, channel its natural inclination to stalk into more regular play sessions, using a toy on a string, fishing-rod toy or something similar (not your hands or feet).

Below: **Your cat may scratch or bite you if it is ill, frightened or if a petting session has gone on too long – learn to recognize when it is becoming agitated.**

You may need to pre-empt attacks by carrying a toy around with you that you can throw if you spot your cat lying in wait. Some owners give the cat's rear a quick squirt with a water pistol to imbue a negative association with this type of behaviour.

PETTING AGGRESSION

Cats often turn on the person who is stroking them. This is dubbed 'petting and biting syndrome' (see also the case history on page 105). It can simply mean that the petting session has gone on too long, and the person has failed to pick up on signs of agitation. In other cases, the attack occurs if the sensitive belly area is touched. Respecting your cat's tolerance for stroking, and learning more about cat body language should help prevent this type of attack. A cat may also scratch if you are trying to put it in a carrier or if you are restraining it.

Pain or illness can also make a cat lash out. Seek advice from a veterinarian if your cat becomes suddenly and inexplicably aggressive.

REDIRECTED AGGRESSION

Sometimes a cat can attack you as a misplaced response to a threat. For example, a cat that catches sight of rival cat through a window may feel fearful and aggressive, and if you go to soothe it, it may vent its aggression against you. This is likely to be a one-off situation, but occasionally the cat may link you with a sense of threat, and continue to attack after the event. Always take extreme care when dealing with a fearful or aggressive cat. Do not try to restrain it unless you are experienced in dealing with cats.

Above: **If your cat is showing signs of defensive aggression – if its fur is fluffed up, for example, or its ears are laid flat against its head – leave it alone, or it may redirect its attack towards you.**

Cat fights

Cats that live together do not always get along and fighting may break out. Understanding why your cats fight is the key to resolving any inter-feline conflict, and making your home a happy place for all your pets.

Even cats that generally get on well are likely to have the odd spat – usually resolved with a hiss and swipe of the paw. Sometimes, though, vicious fighting can break out, and it helps to understand why.

REASONS FOR FIGHTING

Territory is the most common cause of fights between cats. If you bring a new cat into the home and do not introduce it in careful stages (see pages 82–3), the resident cat or cats may well try to see off the interloper. Sometimes, territorial fighting can break out suddenly between two cats who have lived in the same home for a while, often after a break in the relationship (if one has been at the veterinarian's, for example).

Another trigger for fighting is redirected aggression. Just as an agitated cat may attack a person when it sees a strange cat in the garden (see page 141), it may turn its aggression on another cat. The victim might then become fearful, provoking further attacks by the aggressor.

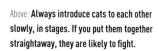

Above: **Always introduce cats to each other slowly, in stages. If you put them together straightaway, they are likely to fight.**

Above: **Even cats that share a home contentedly will have laid claim to their own territory – a favourite chair, perhaps – and may fight to defend it.**

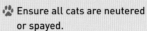
Be aware that cats can resort to subtle forms of aggression, such as blocking another's access to the litter tray or feeding station. Don't assume your cats are getting on well just because you don't see overt signs of aggression.

If your cat becomes vicious suddenly and you can see no reason for it, a medical problem, causing pain and discomfort, may be the trigger. The only thing to do in this case is consult your veterinarian.

DEALING WITH FIGHTS

Never get between two fighting cats. You are likely to get hurt. Instead, throw a pillow between them or make a loud noise – by clashing two saucepans together, for example – to break things up.

If the fighting is frequent, separate the cats. You may want to stage a re-introduction by isolating each cat, and then swapping their scents by passing toys or bedding from one to the other. It can also be helpful to isolate cats in cases of redirected aggression, to give both a chance to forget about the incident. Consider using a pheromone-based spray or diffuser, as these create a more calming atmosphere.

If the problem continues, talk to your veterinarian, who may recommend medication to help resolve the situation. Occasionally, one of the cats may need to be rehomed, though this is obviously a last resort.

Scratching furniture

Cats need to scratch a surface, and if nothing else is available they will vent this urge on your furniture. Fortunately, it is easy to provide an acceptable alternative that will satisfy their natural urges and protect your home from damage.

Scratching, or 'stropping', is a natural behaviour that your cat is compelled to do for two very good reasons. First, it keeps the claws sharp, and second, it is another of the ways that it marks its territory (along with spraying). Not only does scratching leave visible marks for other cats to see, but there are glands in between the claws that deposit the cat's scent on the surface that is clawed. Scratching also helps keep your cat in shape, since the act of stretching helps tone the muscles of the front quarters.

Right: **A scratching post serves an essential function for indoor cats, giving them an outlet for their natural inclination to sharpen their claws and mark their territory.**

SOLUTIONS TO SCRATCHING

Outdoor cats usually have access to a variety of trees and fences that they can claw, so rarely scratch in the home. Cats that are kept inside have the same natural inclination, and need an outlet for it (alongside regular claw trimming). As scratching is a natural behaviour, you should not punish your cat for doing it. Instead, get your cat a sturdy scratching post covered with sisal or a similar material that the cat can dig its claws into. Make sure that it is sturdy because your cat will not use a scratching post that wobbles. It should be tall enough to allow your cat to stretch itself up to its full height (cats stand upright in order to scratch). Or you could try a scratching pad, which can be screwed into the wall. Right-angled pads are also available for corners.

DECLAWING

Some owners have their cats declawed in order to prevent scratching. This involves removing the nail and the last bone of the cat's toe (in human terms, it is like removing the fingers at the last joint). Usually only the front claws are done, since the back claws are rarely used for scratching. There can be post-operative pain and declawing inevitably affects your cat's ability to defend itself should it get outdoors. Declawing is considered inhumane by many and is illegal in some countries of the world, including the UK.

Above: **Scratching is a natural behaviour and, unless you provide it with a suitable alternative, the furniture may be your cat's only option.**

If your cat has been scratching your furniture, place the post next to that area. Make the favoured area of furniture inaccessible by covering it with plastic sheeting, double-sided tape or aluminium foil, which are all off-putting materials to the cat. Encourage your cat to use the scratching post by rubbing it with catnip and by praising any attempts by the cat to claw it. However, do not make the mistake of placing your cat's paws on the post and 'showing' it how to scratch, as this could make your cat refuse to use it.

Once your cat is using the post, move it – a very short distance at a time – to a place that is more to your liking. However, don't place it in an area that is completely out of the way or your cat is likely to shun it and will revert to scratching your furniture again.

Eating plants

It is quite common for cats to nibble at plants. It seems to fulfil a dietary need – but is generally not appreciated by green-fingered cat owners. Providing your cat with its own plants to chew on should solve the problem.

Though cats are carnivores, they do eat plants from time to time. A cat that has access to the outdoors will generally nibble at grass or soft-leaved herbs such as sage and parsley. Cats that are kept indoors may resort to houseplants if there are no more enticing alternatives available.

Below: **Many pet shops sell 'cat grass' seeds, usually a mixture of wheat, rye and oats, so that you can grow your own.**

So long as the plant is not toxic, this is not a cause for concern. However, nibbled leaves do not look good, so this behaviour is sometimes problematic for owners. Cats may also use a pot as a latrine. Covering the surface with pebbles or marbles is a good way to discourage them from doing this as it prevents digging.

PROVIDING AN ALTERNATIVE

Since eating plants is a natural behaviour, you should not try to prevent it. Cats may need this type of vegetable matter to obtain certain nutrients or to induce vomiting to facilitate hairball

removal. If you don't want your cat to chew your houseplants and you can't put them out of reach, the solution is to provide your cat with some of its own. A tray of grass, or a similar cat-friendly plant, is an essential piece of equipment for any indoor cat. It may also enjoy having a pot of catmint to nibble.

It's a good idea to provide indoor-outdoor cats with their own plants as well. Although these cats have plenty of access to plant material outside, it will steer them away from lawns treated with pesticides, which are harmful to cats. Plant a safe selection of favourites such as catmint, parsley and sage in a place that your cat can access easily.

TOXIC PLANTS

Many plants are poisonous for cats. These include household favourites such as azalea, castor-oil plant, dieffenbachia, ivy, philodendron, lily of the valley, amaryllis, poinsettia and cyclamen, as well as the bulbs of flowering plants.

Although adult cats tend to steer clear of poisonous plants, it is safest for your cat if you banish these from the home and garden altogether. Ask your veterinarian for a list of toxic plants that are common in your area. You can also get this information from cat organizations like the Feline Advisory Bureau or the Cat Fanciers' Association.

CHECKLIST
Protecting your plants

As well as providing your cat with its own plants, you can also make your own less enticing. There are many ways to do this:

- Put double-sided tape around the area. Cats hate walking on this, and should be deterred.
- Place the plant pot on a large sheet of aluminium foil or plastic sheeting, which cats dislike.
- Push plant stakes into the soil around the plant. This will block your cat's access to the plant.
- Put a little hot pepper sauce on the leaves.
- Spray cat repellent around the plants (check that it is suitable for your plants).
- Turn your plants into hanging plants that your cat cannot reach.

Wool-eating

Cats are fastidious eaters, but some develop an unusual predilection for chewing wool or other strange materials. This may cause a blockage of the intestines, with potentially fatal consequences.

Cats can develop strange appetites. They may eat wool or other fabrics, or they may like to chew on cardboard. Some cats simply like to lick these or other substances without swallowing them.

The desire to chew and eat inedible substances – a condition known as pica – is not uncommon in cats, but it is seen in some breeds more than others, and mostly in cats that are kept exclusively indoors. Siamese cats in particular seems to have a genetic predisposition towards wool-eating.

Wool-eating must be discouraged because it can lead to intestinal blockage, which may cause serious harm or even death. If your cat stops eating, becomes very lethargic or has diarrhoea, seek immediate advice from your veterinarian.

Left: Wool-eating has been attributed to many diifferent causes, including a nutritional deficiency, an indication of having been weaned too young, a reaction to stress or simply boredom, lack of stimulation and as a substitute for ripping into prey.

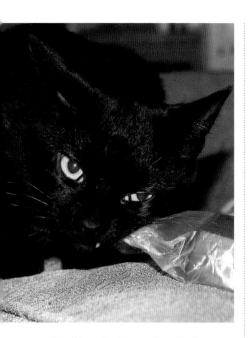

Above: **Cats can develop unusual appetites for a variety of substances: some like to lick photographs or plastic bags; others like to chew on cables.**

CAUSES OF WOOL-EATING

It is not clear why cats start to eat wool. Some animal behaviourists believe that a wool-eating cat may be lacking in certain nutrients, such as iron. Hyperthyroidism (an overactive thyroid gland, which is common in older cats) is another possible cause that should be ruled out by your veterinarian.

The behaviour may a suckling substitute, and a sign that the cat was weaned too early. Wool contains lanolin, which may be a key factor, although it is not clear why. Wool-eating can also be triggered by a stressful event such as moving house, and then develop into a habit.

Another theory is that wool-chewing is a manifestation of natural predatory behaviour. Once a cat has caught its prey, it has to rip into the flesh to eat it. Ordinary cat food does not satisfy this tearing and ripping urge, so the cat finds a substitute. It's possible that boredom and lack of stimulation play a part in this.

TREATMENT

Talk to your veterinarian about your cat's habit. Switching to a high-fibre diet has been known to help in some cases of wool-eating, as has giving naturally textured food that the cat has to tear. Giving your cat constant access to dry food can also help to break the habit. Your veterinarian can give you advice on any recommended supplements.

Consider whether your cat is sufficiently stimulated. Institute regular playtimes if you don't have them already, and incorporate plenty of hunting games (see pages 120–1). Make sure that your cat has a rich environment to explore, with cat trees, perches, hiding places and plenty of toys to chew on. Try hiding dry food around the home, in a variety of hiding places, then encourage the cat to 'hunt' for it. If you think your cat is stressed, take whatever steps possible to reduce this. Using a feline pheromone diffuser or spray may be helpful in this respect.

Most importantly, cut off access to woollen or other targeted items by putting them away and keeping your drawers firmly shut. If your cat cannot get hold of wool, then it cannot harm itself by eating it.

Overgrooming

Cats spend hours grooming themselves, but this natural behaviour can become problematic. Sometimes, cats groom a spot so assiduously that they develop thin or bare patches and the skin may become raw.

Grooming is the cat's way of calming itself down. You have probably noticed your cat nonchalantly attending to its fur at times of stress or indecision. Overgrooming is an extension of this normal displacement activity. It often begins as a response to a stressful event such as moving house. The behaviour then persists when the stress-trigger is no longer relevant, and becomes frequent and habitual to the point of obsessiveness. Generally a bald spot will develop, and sometimes the skin will also become raw. The most common places for a cat to overgroom are the inside of the legs and the abdomen. Oriental cats, which are naturally more nervous by disposition, are more likely to engage in overgrooming than other breeds.

Right: **Overgrooming can start as a reaction to stress, and become an obsessive-compulsive behaviour that continues long after the original trigger has been forgotten.**

MEDICAL CAUSES

If your cat develops a thin or bald spot, you should consider medical causes first. Ringworm, a fungal infection, is a possible cause of baldness. Parasites such as mites or fleas may lead the cat to repeatedly bite and scratch, which can also cause baldness. Poor nutrition and food allergies are other triggers.

Your veterinarian will be able to diagnose any medical problem. Skin scrapings may be taken to check for the presence of parasites, and blood tests will reveal any hormonal imbalance. Your veterinarian may also recommend an elimination diet (in which a particular food is excluded from the diet, then re-introduced to check for reactions), or corticosteroids, which are helpful in cases of allergy.

DEALING WITH OVERGROOMING

If the overgrooming is due to stress, do what you can to address the underlying cause. For example, if your cat is unhappy because of another cat in the household, separate and gradually reintroduce them to each other, using the method described on page 80. Consider whether anything else may have changed in your cat's environment or routine, and if so, and if you can, change it back.

Stick to a fixed routine of mealtimes and playtimes – nervous cats are happier if they know what is happening and when. Use a pheromone spray or plug-in diffuser to make your home more soothing for

Above: **Your cat's environment can determine whether it is happy or not. All cats need perches, hiding places and space to look out of a window.**

your cat. If you spot your cat biting or scratching at the bald area, distract it and offer playtime. An aquarium or feline DVD is a helpful way of distracting your cat from its habit.

Consider whether your home is enriching enough for your cat and whether you are giving it enough attention. You may want to invest in some more toys. Make sure that your cat has hiding places, perches, space to look out of a window and so on (see pages 92–3).

If the situation does not resolve itself, you will need to consult your veterinarian. It may be that mood-stabilizing medication is needed to relive your cat's anxiety.

A healthy cat

It is important for all cat owners to understand that cats hide signs of illness very well. This tendency to dissemble is a legacy of their past: no wild cat wants to exhibit any sign of weakness. This chapter shows you how to keep a close eye on your cat so that you pick up on problems straight away, even when your cat is pretending all is well. There is advice on preventive health care, including vaccinations, neutering and parasite control, as well as pointers on choosing the second most important person in your cat's life – the veterinarian.

Cats generally live long and healthy lives, but they are prone to certain ailments. So this chapter contains information on common sicknesses and treatments, as well as advice on the tricky business of giving your cat medication. There is also a guide to caring for your cat at times when it needs additional care, such as during pregnancy or in the final years of its life.

Choosing a veterinarian

Veterinarians, like family doctors, have different styles and attitudes to health care. It is important to choose someone that you feel comfortable dealing with and who you can trust with your cat's health needs.

Choose a veterinarian before you really need one – don't wait until an emergency occurs. Your veterinarian will be an important person in your cat's life, providing regular check-ups, vaccinations and boosters, as well as medical treatment should it become ill. It is essential that your veterinarian is someone that you trust and consider competent.

Remember that veterinarians can work with many kinds of animals, from reptiles to livestock. Most specialize in particular types or species, and it makes sense to choose one that has an interest in cats. Many veterinarians work in group practices, which have the obvious benefit that they can consult each other for help with diagnosis. A good solo practitioner should have links with other veterinarians for the same purpose. If you register with a group practice, ask if you can see the same veterinarian each time so that he or she can get to know you and your cat.

FINDING YOUR VETERINARIAN
The best way to find a veterinarian is through recommendation. If you bought your pet from a local breeder, then it is worth asking who they use. A good breeder is likely to have chosen their veterinarian carefully,

Left: Some veterinarians have a particular inerest in complementary therapies, such as homeopathy or chiropractic medicine. This may be an important factor in your choice of practice.

and should be able to provide a reference. If you have sourced your cat from a cat-rescue society, then the staff there are likely to know the local veterinarians, and may recommend one to you. Cat-owning friends and neighbours with whom you share similar attitudes towards pets may also be able to point you in the right direction.

Always take the time to visit a veterinary practice before registering your pet. This allows you to assess the staff and facilities. A good veterinarian should be prepared to show you the facilities and to talk to you about your pet's needs. Choose someone who is happy to answer any questions you may have.

Above: **Whether you get a recommendation or find your veterinarian through the phone book or internet, do your research and check that he or she is right for you and your pet.**

CHECKLIST
The right veterinarian for you

In order to select a veterinarian best suited to your needs, consider the following:

- Is the practice within reasonable travelling distance?
- Are there good parking facilities?
- Is the clinic well-organized and clean?
- Are the reception staff courteous, caring and efficient?
- Do the opening times suit you?
- Is the clinic by appointment only, drop-in, or both?
- What is the provision for emergency care after hours?
- Does the veterinarian do home visits?
- How many veterinarians work in the practice?

- What are the fees?
- If it's a group practice, can you choose a particular veterinarian?
- Is the veterinarian a member of a feline advisory organization?
- Does the veterinarian have links with specialists for difficult cases?
- What is the veterinarian's attitude towards complementary therapies?
- Does the veterinarian have a particular interest or specialism?
- Are X-rays, ultrasounds and other diagnostic tests carried out on the premises or do you have to be referred to a specialist centre?

Vaccinations

Vaccinations play an important part in keeping your cat healthy. Talk to your veterinarian about what vaccinations are necessary for your cat because this can vary, depending on your location and the circumstances in which your cat lives.

WHY VACCINATE?

Routine vaccinations have had a huge impact on cutting the incidence of feline diseases. Some ('core vaccinations') are recommended for all cats, while others ('non-core vaccinations') are advised only for cats whose lifestyle or environment puts them at risk of exposure to the disease in question. Discuss what is appropriate with your veterinarian.

Kittens are usually given a first, all-in-one vaccination at eight to nine weeks, with a booster at 12 weeks

Below: **A kitten should have its first vaccinations at eight or nine weeks, before you take it home.**

(the rabies shot is also given then). Another booster vaccination is given one year later, to ensure a good level of continuing immunity. Cats should be in a good state of health when given vaccinations, and your veterinarian should do a routine examination of your cat before giving the shot for this reason.

SIDE-EFFECTS

Vaccination, like any medical intervention, carries a risk of side-effects, but most experts agree that the benefits far outweigh the risks. One recent concern is that a small number of cats have developed a tumour at the injection site. This complication is more common in the USA than the UK, and is thought to be linked to the rabies and FeLV vaccinations. Discuss this, and any other concerns about side-effects, with your veterinarian, who can explain the steps being taken to minimize the risk.

CHECKLIST
Which vaccinations?

Core vaccinations protect your cat against the following common and highly contagious diseases:

- **FELINE PANLEUKOPENIA** (also known as **FPV, FELINE INFECTIOUS ENTERITIS** and **FELINE PAROVIRUS**) This is an extremely contagious virus which causes severe gastroenteritis. It can be fatal.
- **FELINE HERPESVIRUS (FHV** or **FELINE RHINOTRACHEITIS)** and **FELINE CALCIVIRUS (FCV)** These viruses are responsible for most cases of 'cat flu'. Symptoms include sneezing, nasal and oral discharge, coughing, conjunctivitis, mouth ulcers and fever. Cat flu can be fatal.
- **RABIES** This is usually fatal, and is easily spread from animal to human. It is a core vaccination in countries where rabies is endemic. British cats do not need to be vaccinated against rabies unless travelling abroad.

Depending on your cat's circumstances, you may also be advised to give other vaccinations. These include:

- **FELINE CHLAMYDOPHILOSIS** This bacterium causes conjunctivitis and sometimes a nasal discharge. It is passed on by direct contact between cats, and vaccination is often recommended for cats living in multi-cat households.
- **FELINE LEUKAEMIA VIRUS (FELV)** This virus is transmitted by direct contact between cats, and is usually fatal within three years of diagnosis. Vaccination is usually recommended for cats with access to the outdoors, but check with your veterinarian.

Until recently, adult cats have routinely received booster vaccinations annually. However, there is growing evidence that the effect of the vaccinations lasts longer than one year, and new information suggests that three-yearly boosters of the core vaccinations (excluding rabies) is sufficient for most cats. Again, your veterinarian will help you to make the appropriate decision to protect your cat's health.

Above: **Not every cat needs every vaccination. Your veterinarian should take into account your cat's age, health and circumstances when planning its vaccination programme.**

Neutering your cat

Neutering, like vaccination, is a preventative medical procedure that helps safeguard your cat's health. It also improves aspects of its behaviour. Unless you plan to breed from your cat, most experts agree that you should have it neutered at an early age.

Neutering your cat is good for its health, and reduces the overall incidence of unwanted kittens. There are clear health and behaviour benefits, too. Neutered (spayed) females are protected against diseases such as pyometra (infection of the womb) and some cancers. As a result, neutered females tend to live much longer than unneutered ones.

Male cats fight less if they are neutered, so they incur fewer injuries and wound-related infections. Neutering also reduces the risk that your cat will pick up serious diseases such as feline immunodeficiency virus (FIV) or feline leukaemia virus (FeLV), which are spread by cat bites.

Owners also benefit from having their cat neutered. An unneutered cat will have some unappealing habits when it is on heat: an unneutered female calls continually for a mate, and is likely to attract males who will fight, spray and caterwaul. An unneutered tom can be aggressive to other cats, and is much more likely to spray in the home. Neutered males are much less territorial and tend to have sweeter and more affectionate dispositions.

Left: **Neutered males are more likely to become overweight since they have a much reduced desire to roam. You will need to cut down on your cat's food, and to keep a careful eye on its shape.**

WHEN TO NEUTER

Owners used to be told to neuter their cats at around six months of age. However, some cats mature as early as four months. Many experts now recommend neutering at four months for this reason, and rescue organizations are neutering stray kittens from seven weeks with no apparent ill effects. Neutering should only be carried out by a licensed veterinarian.

NEUTERING PROCEDURE

In the male, the procedure is carried out through small incisions in the scrotum, and involves removing the testicles and tying the spermatic cords. No stitches are needed. Since a general anaesthetic is used, the cat should not be fed from the evening before the procedure. You can bring your cat home the same day.

Spaying a female involves removing the ovaries and uterus through an incision in the abdomen or flank (which is shaved to prevent infection). The procedure is done under general anaesthetic, so no food should be given from the evening beforehand. The cat usually comes home the same day, and the stitches are removed a week later.

A cat may be drowsy after neutering, and should be placed in a warm, comfortable place to recover; give it access to water, food and a litter tray. Males usually recover in a few hours, while females may take a couple of days to recuperate. Contact your veterinarian if your cat is unusually quiet or if it starts to worry at the stitches, or if there are unusual symptoms. Be sure to keep a female cat indoors until the stitches have been removed.

Below: **To avoid the risk of unwanted pregnancy, a cat should be neutered before its first season. Many experts recommend that this is done at four months.**

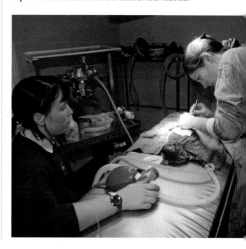

Routine health checks

Signs of ill health can be subtle in cats, so you need to be vigilant. Checking over your cat regularly will help ensure that you don't miss any worrying symptoms; the sooner you get a sick cat to the veterinarian's, the better its chances of recovery.

Talk to your veterinarian about what is appropriate for your cat in terms of health checks. An annual check-up is sufficient for most cats, but elderly cats may need more frequent visits. At these check-ups, the veterinarian will look for signs of parasites, check your cat's breathing and pulse rate, and talk to you about your cat's habits. Dental scaling and polishing may be carried out, which helps keep your cat's mouth and gums healthy. If necessary, the veterinarian will clip your cat's nails.

As important as a check-up at the veterinarian's is, you should not rely on this alone. Keep an eye out for behaviour that could be a symptom of illness, such as toileting outside the litter tray, loss of appetite or lethargy.

CHECKING YOUR CAT AT HOME

It is a good idea to do a systematic health check once a week or so. This may help you to pick up on problems or abnormalites. It is also a good way of getting your cat used to being examined, which will help with veterinarian visits. If your cat objects, do one area of the body at a time. Reward your cat for putting up with this by playing games, giving food treats and stroking it.

It is a good idea to record your observations in a book as this will help you to take account of subtle changes that occur over time. See your veterinarian if you notice any

Left: **An annual check-up by the veterinarian is an important aspect of any preventative health programme. It is also a chance for you to buy the right worming and anti-flea products for your cat.**

abnormalities. Take your notebook with you as your observations may help with diagnosis and treatment.

General condition

First, consider how your cat seems overall. Is it active and alert? Is it eating and drinking as usual? A change in appetite or drinking habits can indicate a health problem and should be reported to a veterinarian. Sluggishness, being withdrawn and a lack of interest in grooming can also be signs of ill health, as can changes in urination or bowel movements, changes in sleep patterns, or sudden aggression in a normally friendly cat.

Next, examine your cat's posture and gait. Is your cat holding itself and walking normally? Stiffness may indicate problems with the joints, while limping may suggest an injury or fracture, a thorn stuck in the foot, infection in the foot or arthritis. Internal injuries may also cause your cat to move around less, and to shy from your touch.

Above: **Nobody knows your cat like you do, and you are in the ideal position to spot subtle signs of illness such as loss of appetite, increased thirst or unusual behaviours.**

BASIC INSTINCT **Why cats may hide signs of illness**

Illness in a cat is not always easy to spot. One reason for this is that cats often try to act as if they are not ill. This behaviour is a throwback to their wild ancestry, to a time when a sick-looking cat would make an obvious target for predators. For its own protection, a cat will try to look healthy, or otherwise hide away. This is why a normally sociable cat can become withdrawn when it is unwell.

Body

Stroke your hand over your cat's body, feeling for any areas of heat, swelling or other abnormalities that may indicate an injury, bite, abscess or other problem. Start with the head, face, jaw and throat, then move on to the neck, back, sides and chest. Feel around the hips, groin and legs, flexing the joints. Then check the feet, examining the claw pads for signs of infection and the claws for length (see page 108), and finish with the tail. Any flinching or cries from your cat may indicate pain.

Abdomen

Gently press your hands into the abdomen, starting just below the chest and working your way towards the rear. As you palpate, check for any lumps, hardness or swelling. See your veterinarian if you find anything that is not usually there, or if your cat is breathing strangely or cries out.

Coat

A healthy cat has a soft, glossy coat. Dullness, thinness or abnormally raised fur is often a sign of illness and should be reported to your veterinarian. Check your cat's coat for parasites and bare patches. Part the hair and check that the skin looks clean and that there is no black dust (a sign of fleas), nits (the white eggs of a louse), or dandruff (which may indicate fur mites).

Left: **Giving your cat a physical examination needn't take long, but will alert you to problems early on. Choose a time when your cat is calm, and be gentle.**

Eyes

The eyes should be bright and clear, and free from discharge (wipe away with damp cotton wool). The pupils should be the same size and the third eyelid should be retracted. Cloudiness or redness is abnormal and needs swift veterinary attention, as do any fight injuries in this area.

Ears and nose

The ears should be clean and dry, and the ear canal should be clean and odour-free. Clear wax is normal, but smelly or dirty ears need veterinary attention. Very hot ears can indicate a high temperature. The nose should be clean and moist with no discharge.

Mouth

The gums should be pale pink and moist, and the teeth white and well-rooted, with no breakages. There should be no odour, inflammation, swelling or build-up of tartar around the base of the teeth – see your veterinarian if you spot any of these. Check for lumps around the neck, and take your cat to the veterinarian if you find any.

Weight

Check your cat's weight regularly, and see your veterinarian if there is a change of more than 225 grams (8 oz) in an adult cat, or if there is a sudden loss or gain.

Breathing

Listen carefully to your cat's breathing. Noisy, laboured or rapid breathing (other than natural panting) is abnormal, and needs immediate veterinary attention.

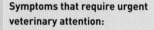

CHECKLIST
When to call for help

Symptoms that require urgent veterinary attention:

- Blood in urine, faeces or vomit
- High temperature
- Vomiting with diarrhoea
- Repeated vomiting or severe diarrhoea
- Bleeding from the genitals
- Straining to pass urine
- Shallow or laboured breathing
- Seizure, collapse or balance problems
- Severe pain or discomfort
- Involvement in a traffic accident (even if the cat seems fine)
- Ingesting a toxic substance or plant

External parasites

Various parasites such as fleas, mites and ticks can live on your cat. They can cause irritation, and some more serious problems. Modern treatments have made it relatively easy to prevent and treat external parasites.

FLEAS

Fleas are the commonest cause of skin problems in cats, and they also transmit tapeworms (see page 166). If your cat has fleas, you may spot small black dust (flea droppings) in its coat and your cat may scratch persistently. You and any other people who share the home with your cat may have itchy bites, especially on the ankles.

Below: **Frequent scratching may be a sign that your cat has fleas. You may also spot black flea dust when you check your cat's fur.**

To check for fleas, comb the cat's fur with a flea comb, collecting any droppings on a damp tissue. Squeeze the dust between two sides of the tissue. Flea droppings contain blood and will stain the tissue red-brown.

Treat an affected cat with a spot-on product recommended by your veterinarian. You will need to treat its environment, too, to prevent re-infestation. Wash the cat's bedding and vacuum all carpets and soft furnishings (dispose of the vacuum bag straight away). Use a long-acting

household spray, and treat all soft furnishings, carpet and any gaps between floorboards and around skirting boards. Repeated treatment may be needed to eradicate fleas from the home, and it is best to seek advice from your veterinarian for effective and safe control.

It is easier to prevent fleas than it is to treat them. A spot-on treatment can be applied once a month; this will also prevent tapeworms. Practising good hygiene is also important. Vacuum the areas where your cat sleeps every day and wash its bedding once a week.

EAR MITES AND OTHER MITES

Ear mites are easily passed from one cat to another, and cause severe irritation. A cat with ear mites is likely to scratch repeatedly at its ears and shake its head. The ears will look dirty. See your veterinarian, who will clean the ear and prescribe a topical treatment. Use the medication for as long as directed, even if the problem seems to clear up sooner, otherwise it may recur. Other types of mite that can affect a cat include fur mites, which may be indicated by excessive dandruff. Again, seek advice from your veterinarian.

TICKS

A tick is a blood-sucking parasite that causes soreness and can transmit disease. It burrows its head into the skin, leaving the body exposed (you may notice the small bump when petting your cat). Your veterinarian can remove the tick. If you want to remove it yourself, put on gloves to

WARNING

Since cats are highly sensitive to parasiticides, it is best to obtain anti-flea products from your veterinarian, particularly if you have a kitten, or an elderly or ill cat. Use only products specially formulated for felines; dog flea products may contain permethrin, which can be fatal to cats. Always follow the manufacturer's guidelines carefully, and do not use more than one product, because it can lead to overdose.

protect yourself from infection, then swab the tick with surgical alcohol, grasp close to the cat's skin with tweezers or a special tick-remover, and pull out in one piece without twisting. Place the tick in a jar of alcohol to kill it. Ticks can be prevented with some flea-control products.

Right: **A little clear wax in the ear is quite normal, but if your cat's ears seem dirty, then ear mites are the likely culprit.**

Internal parasites

It's very common for cats to harbour internal parasites, and these can be hard to spot. There are often no obvious signs, but heavy infestation may cause weight loss, vomiting or diarrhoea, and a general failure to thrive.

Regular worming will keep your kitten or cat free from internal parasites. Worming products are available over the counter, but it is best to consult your veterinarian about a worming programme for your cat because this will vary according to its age and circumstances.

TAPEWORMS

Tapeworms are long, flat worms. Cats usually get them by eating infected fleas during grooming. Routine flea treatment is necessary to prevent your cat from becoming infected.

If your cat has a tapeworm, it will expel small segments containing the worm eggs in its faeces. These look like grains of rice and can be seen around the cat's anus or in its bed. Tapeworms do not seem to affect cats very much unless they are heavily infested, when they may suffer diarrhoea.

ROUNDWORMS

Roundworms are thin and about 7–18 centimetres (3–7 in) long. Cats may ingest them from infected soil (normally through grooming) or from infected rodents. Pregnancy reactivates dormant larvae in the mother cat's body, and the worms are passed in her milk to her kittens.

Left: **If you have more than one cat, parasites may be passed from one to the other easily. All the cats in the household usually need to be treated if one is diagnosed with parasites.**

Often there are no symptoms, but a kitten or cat that is heavily affected may have a dull coat and pot-bellied abdomen, and may suffer diarrhoea or vomiting; it may also expel worms. Occasionally, intestinal blockage or pneumonia results. Kittens should be routinely wormed as a preventative measure when young.

HOOKWORM

These small, bloodsucking parasites can affect cats of all ages (they are rare in the UK). They attach themselves to the lining of the intestine and can cause anaemia or even death. Cats get them by walking on infected soil; the worms penetrate the skin, or the cat may ingest them by licking its paws. An affected cat is usually thin and its fur becomes dull and unhealthy-looking. It may have diarrhoea that contains blood.

HEARTWORM

These worms are transmitted by mosquitoes, and live in the heart and lungs. An affected cat may suffer vomiting or loss of appetite, coughing and breathing difficulties, though symptoms vary. Sudden death may occur. Heartworm is a problem only in certain countries, and is not present in the UK. They can be difficult to diagnose and treatment is based on relieving symptoms.

TOXOPLASMOSIS

This is one of the most common parasitic diseases in both animals and humans. Toxoplasmosis is caused by microscopic organisms that live in the intestines. It is hard to tell whether your cat has been infected since most have no symptoms. However, severe infection may cause breathing difficulties, weight loss and high temperature (in which case you should take it to the veterinarian). Cats become infected by eating infected prey or raw or undercooked meat; avoid giving your cat raw meat to reduce the risk of infection. Eggs are passed in the cat's faeces for up to several weeks after infection and become infective only after 24 hours; humans can contract toxoplasmosis by handling contaminated soil or litter as well as (more commonly) by eating raw or undercooked meat. Toxoplasmosis does not usually have serious effects on healthy people (many people do not realize that they have been infected), but pregnant women and those with compromised immune systems are at risk, so should take precautionary measures. For example, they should wear gloves when gardening, cover children's sandpits to prevent cats from using them, and avoid emptying a cat's litter tray, as well as refraining from eating raw, undercooked or cured meat. Ideally the cat's litter tray should be changed at least once a day (by someone else). To set your mind at rest, you can check whether you have previously been infected with toxoplasmosis (and are therefore immune) by having a blood test.

Common problems

Even the best cared-for cat will have health problems from time to time. Seeking veterinary treatment at the first sign of trouble is the best way to ensure that illnesses do not become chronic and to confirm they are not a sign of something more serious.

Cats have a reputation as being easy to care for – which is generally true. However, they may be affected by a wide range of health issues.

VOMITING

Occasional vomiting in cats is not usually a cause for concern. It may be a sign of motion sickness, or the presence of hairballs or other foreign matter. In mild cases, give water but withhold food for 12–24 hours, then gradually introduce light food, such as cooked chicken. Make sure your cat has access to water at all times.

Prolonged vomiting may indicate an obstruction in the intestines, which can be life-threatening. Immediate veterinary help should be sought in this case, or if you suspect your cat has swallowed wool or thread (which can easily cause an obstruction). Blood in the vomit, recurrent vomiting, severe vomiting, or vomiting with diarrhoea or fever also require swift veterinary treatment. There are many causes of vomiting, such as metabolic disease, tumour, stomach ulcers and infection. Treatment will depend on the underlying cause.

Right: **Toileting problems – such as straining while passing urine – are a common sign of illness, some of which may be life-threatening.**

DIARRHOEA

Most cats will suffer a bout of diarrhoea from time to time, often as the result of overeating, of consuming something that does not agree with their digestion, or of stress. The problem usually clears up quickly. Give your cat water, but withhold food for 12–24 hours, then introduce easy-to-digest food such as cooked chicken. If the diarrhoea continues, consult your veterinarian.

Prolonged diarrhoea or diarrhoea with blood in the stools, fever or lethargy requires urgent attention. There are many possible causes, including inflammatory bowel disease, worms, dietary intolerance, infectious diseases such as giardia, hyperthyroidism or tumour. Your veterinarian may wish to do various tests. Treatment depends on the cause. A cat with chronic diarrhoea can easily become dehydrated and may require hydrating treatment.

Above: **Dehydration is a risk if your cat is vomiting, has diarrhoea or has heatstroke. A good check for this is to gently pull the skin at the back of the cat's neck. If it does not spring instantly back into place, hydration treatment is required.**

CONSTIPATION

Cats normally expel faeces between one and four times a day. If a cat is constipated, it will go less often than normal and may make repeated trips to the litter tray, and strain while trying to expel faeces. The faeces may become impacted, and the abdomen may be distended. Simple cases can be treated with laxatives or an enema (under anaesthetic). Sometimes surgery is needed.

URINARY TRACT PROBLEMS

Cats are prone to problems in the urinary tract. Pain when in the litter box, blood in the urine, increased urination or accidents in a usually house-trained cat are all common signs and should be reported to your veterinarian straight away. In serious cases, there may be a blockage in the urethra, and an affected cat may cry in pain and strain without managing to urinate. This problem needs urgent attention as it may cause kidney damage and even death.

Elderly cats can suffer kidney failure. The signs are increased urination, increased thirst, as well as bad breath and weight loss. See your veterinarian for a definite diagnosis, and for help in managing the condition through diet.

Left: **An obese cat will find it hard to carry out activities such as walking, jumping and grooming. It is also at greater risk of a variety of health problems.**

an obese cat it is hard to feel the hip bones and may not be possible to feel the ribs at all; the cat's abdomen may also be distended. Simple activities such as walking and grooming can be difficult.

You should monitor your cat's weight (see pages 102–3), reduce food treats (not meals) and encourage activity if you notice that your cat is getting heavier. Weight gain can have a medical cause, so see your veterinarian if there's no improvement after a couple of weeks.

RINGWORM

Ringworm is a fungicidal infection, not a worm. It is highly contagious, and can affect humans, especially children. An affected cat may have hair loss and round, red and scaly patches on its skin, which are very itchy. Some cats show no symptoms but should be treated if they have been in contact with a cat that has ringworm.

Take your cat to the veterinarian for a definite diagnosis, and for advice on treatment. It takes time to rid a cat of ringworm. Usually both oral and topical treatments are used, and the cat's fur may be clipped to

OBESITY

A third of pet cats are overweight or obese. Carrying extra weight puts strain on the cat's joints and internal organs, and may lead to a variety of health problems. These include heart disease, diabetes, urinary conditions and arthritis.

A healthy cat has a thin layer of fat over its ribs and hip bones, and can walk and groom itself easily. In

Above: **Clean your cat's teeth regularly with a special toothbrush to prevent mouth problems. Be aware that bad breath may be a sign of serious disease such as kidney failure so take your cat to the veterinarian's for a check-up if bad breath persists.**

make treatment easier. The household will need to be thoroughly cleaned to eradicate spores and so prevent re-infection. It is helpful to confine the cat to one easy-to-clean room while treatment is ongoing. Your veterinarian will advise you on the most effective products.

MOUTH PROBLEMS

A cat's breath should not smell, so odour in the mouth should be investigated by a veterinarian. Possible causes include a build up of tartar (brownish stains at the base of the teeth), food stuck between the teeth, gingivitis (inflammation of the gums), ulceration or rotten teeth. Bad breath can also be a sign of kidney failure or other diseases. Treatment will depend on the underlying cause, but you should clean your cat's teeth regularly to help prevent mouth problems.

CASE HISTORY
The obese cat

Anne had two cats. The female, Jessie, was outgoing and active. Miles, on the other hand, was 'a scaredy-cat', who did not like going outside and exploring. Miles became noticeably overweight after he was neutered, and Anne's veterinarian recommended restricting his diet.

Anne immediately stopped giving Miles food treats in addition to his meals. Since Miles was fond of eating out of Jessie's bowl as well as his own, she fed them in separate places – and cleared away uneaten food straight away. She also started daily playtime sessions with Miles, encouraging him to 'hunt' for the dried food that he loved. Miles became more active and slowly returned to a healthier shape.

Above: **Cloudiness in the eyes is a sign of cataracts. Don't leave this untreated, since it can lead to glaucoma and blindness.**

CONJUNCTIVITIS AND EYE PROBLEMS

Conjunctivitis is inflammation of the conjunctiva (the outer layer of the eye), and is common in cats. It can be the result of injury or irritation by a foreign body in the eye, or it can be a symptom of cat flu, chlamydiosis or other diseases. Treatment is usually with antibiotic eye drops.

All eye problems, however slight, should be treated promptly, since sight loss can be rapid and is usually irreversible. Cats are prone to many of the eye conditions that people suffer, including cataracts and glaucoma. Minor eye problems can also indicate serious disease elsewhere in the body.

ABSCESSES

An abscess is a pus-filled swelling under the skin. It usually starts with a bite or scratch wound, which then becomes infected. Take your cat to the veterinarian if you suspect an abscess, which may cause it to limp or become feverish. The abscess will be drained, and antibiotics may be prescribed for your cat.

DERMATITIS

A red rash on your cat's skin, generally known as dermatitis, may be the result of an allergic reaction to fleas or to a particular food. It is exacerbated by scratching. Your veterinarian will suggest treatment to alleviate the irritation.

TUMOURS

Cats – especially elderly cats – are prone to tumours, which may be benign or malignant (cancerous). The main sign is a swelling under the skin. Other symptoms of cancer include unexplained bleeding, breathing difficulties, and intestinal problems (depending on the location of the tumour).

Your veterinarian may need to carry out diagnostic blood tests, biopsies and other investigations. Treatments include surgery, radiotherapy and chemotherapy, and your cat may need to be referred to a specialist centre for these.

VIRUSES

Cats are susceptible to some nasty viruses, such as the ones that cause feline leukaemia virus (FeLV) and feline panleukopenia (feline infectious enteritis). Regular vaccination will protect your cat from these, but young kittens and wild cats are at risk. You should always

ensure a new cat is free from these diseases before introducing it into your household.

Cat flu is common in unvaccinated cats, and can affect those that have been vaccinated. Feline herpesvirus (FHV) can be life-threatening and symptoms may become chronic. Feline calcivirus (FCV) is usually milder but some kittens develop lameness after infection. Most cats recover from cat flu, but become carriers, passing the disease to other cats.

Feline infectious peritonitis (FIP) usually affects kittens and is invariably fatal. There is a vaccine but it cannot be given until a cat is 16 weeks and – since older cats are rarely affected by this disease – many experts do not believe that it should be given routinely.

Above: An outdoor cat is much more likely to come into contact with serious viruses such as feline leukaemia virus (FeLV), which is often passed through cat bites. See your veterinarian to discuss vaccination if your cat has access to the outdoors.

Feline immunodeficiency virus (FIV) is the feline equivalent to the HIV virus. It is not transferable to humans. Affected cats have a compromised immune system, leaving them susceptible to infections and diseases such as cancer. If your cat is diagnosed with FIV, you and your veterinarian will need to keep a close eye on it, so that health problems and infections can be treated early on – cats can live for years with FIV. You should keep an infected cat indoors, both to protect it from infections and to protect other cats from FIV.

Giving medication

All owners will have to adminster medication to their cats at some point in their lives, either as a preventative measure or to clear up a health problem. Learning the techniques will make the process easier on you both.

Wait until your cat is relaxed before giving medication. It is easier to get someone else to hold the cat, but if you have to do the job alone, wrap your cat in a towel so you don't get scratched. Always follow your veterinarian's instructions, and do not stop the medication or change the dosage without consulting a

Below: **Always give a cat something to swallow after administering a pill. Certain medications may cause damage to the oesophagus if the pill gets stuck, and it will also ensure that the pill travels down to the stomach quickly.**

professional. Don't use medication that's past its use-by date, and take unused medications to the surgery for safe disposal.

ADMINISTERING A PILL OR LIQUID MEDICINE

Take hold of your cat's head from above, so that your thumb is pointing down one side and your fingers down the other. Tilt the head back, and use the index finger of your other hand to lever the mouth open. Place the pill as far back in the mouth as possible, then close. It may help if you stroke

CARING FOR A SICK CAT

A sick cat may need time to recuperate. Put it in a quiet and comfortable place, keeping other animals and children away. Make a temporary bed by cutting down one side of a cardboard box and lining with newspaper and a towel. Give your cat a lukewarm, covered hot-water bottle to help it keep warm. Place food and water nearby, and a litter tray a little distance away.

Right: **When giving eye-drops, warm the bottle by rolling it in your hand first. The experience will be less uncomfortable for your cat if the drops are at body temperature.**

the cat's throat. Give your cat a food treat as a reward and to help the pill move down the oesophagus. Alternatively, syringe a little water into the cat's mouth.

You will also need to use a syringe if the medication is in liquid form. Hold the cat's head as you would when giving a pill, but lift its lip and push the syringe gently past the teeth into the mouth. Release the medication slowly, pausing to allow your cat to swallow.

DISPENSING A SPOT-ON LOTION

Administering a spot-on lotion is simpler than giving a pill. Part the hair at the back of the neck to expose the skin, then apply the lotion. You may need to apply it to two different locations, depending on the manufacturer's instructions.

GIVING EAR DROPS

Hold your cat and make sure that it is calm by stroking, or by speaking to it. Administer the recommended number of drops using the dropper provided, then massage the base of the ear. Your cat will shake its head vigorously, so use a cloth to protect your clothing. The dose is set to take account of the shaking, so don't give more than directed.

GIVING EYE DROPS

Calm your cat, then hold its head steady with one hand under the chin. Bring the bottle above the eye from behind and apply the right number of drops. If applying ointment, gently pull back the lower eyelid and squeeze out a small amount of ointment onto the edge of the eyelid. Close the eye briefly. Make sure that there is no contact between the eye and the bottle or tube.

First aid for cats

Emergencies are rare, but there may be times when some basic feline first aid is necessary. Your prompt action could save your cat's life. Do not offer an injured cat anything to eat or drink since it may require an anaesthetic.

Your cat will be treated more quickly if you take it straight to the surgery. Lift it carefully without bending or twisting (wrap it in a towel if it is fearful or aggressive). Place it gently in a cardboard box containing soft bedding. Keep an injured cat warm.

BASIC FIRST AID

Always have your veterinarian's number to hand in case of an emergency. Call straight away: the staff may give you advice on what immediate action to take.

Below: **Keep an injured cat warm when taking it to the veterinarian's. An injured cat may lash out so wrap it in a towel before picking it up.**

Fights

Clean minor wounds with lukewarm salty water. Make an appointment with your veterinarian if your cat has been in a fight since antibiotics may be needed.

Falls and road accidents

Take your cat straight to the veterinarian – it may have internal injuries. Keep the cat horizontal; make a 'stretcher' from a coat or rug and gently slide the cat onto it, supporting its body at all times. Keep the head a little lower than the legs to encourage blood flow to the brain.

Burns

Run the area under cold water for five minutes, then call a veterinarian. Wrap the cat in a towel to keep warm.

Drowning

Hold the cat by the hindlegs to drain water from its lungs (you may need to swing gently from side to side). Resuscitate if the cat is not breathing (see right). Keep your cat warm and take it to the veterinarian's even if it seems to be recovered.

Wounds

Clean superficial scrapes with saline solution and cotton wool. Staunch bleeding by applying gentle pressure with a sterile pad. Do not press on penetrating objects. Do not splint a fracture or apply a tourniquet.

Stings

If possible, pull out the sting by grasping the base with tweezers. Contact your veterinarian immediately if your cat is stung in the mouth or throat because the subsequent swelling may affect its breathing.

Shock

A cat in shock has irregular, shallow breathing and pale gums. It may or may not be conscious. Place the cat on its side, extend the head, keep warm, and elevate the hindquarters so that blood flows to the brain. Take your cat to the veterinarian as soon as possible.

Coat contamination

Stop the cat from licking its coat by wrapping it in a thick towel. Take to the veterinarian for bathing.

Poisoning

Take your cat immediately to the veterinarian together with a sample of the poison packaging or plant.

CHECKLIST
Resuscitating a cat

If your cat is unconscious and unresponsive, place it on its side and lift the chin to open up the airway. Check that your cat is breathing by holding a piece of tissue in front of its nose (it should flutter). If not, you will have to do artificial resuscitation. Seek emergency veterinary advice as soon as possible. The basic process is as follows:

- Open the cat's mouth, pull the tongue forwards and clear any obstructions from mouth and nose. Remove the collar. Lift the cat upright.
- Close the mouth, place your mouth over the cat's nose and blow into it for two seconds to inflate the lungs (do not over-inflate). Pause, then repeat ten times every minute until the cat breathes normally.
- If there is no heartbeat, press on the chest to a depth of two centimetres

(¾ in) just behind the forelegs at one-second intervals. Give two breaths to every 15 chest pushes. Check your cat's heart is beating every 15 seconds. (Listen on the left side of the chest, just behind the cat's elbow; you can also feel for a pulse here or inside the cat's hind leg where it meets the groin.)
- Keep going until veterinary help arrives, your cat's heart starts to beat, or you feel it is beyond recovery.

Other therapies

Increasing numbers of veterinarians now offer complementary therapies as well as conventional treatment. These can be helpful for certain conditions, but the medical problem must be correctly diagnosed before any complementary therapy is given.

If complementary healing interests you, find a veterinarian who is sympathetic to this approach and work closely with him or her to choose the best treatment for your pet. In general, complementary practitioners take a holistic view of the animal, considering all aspects of its wellbeing rather than focusing on a particular condition or symptom. Complementary therapies can be beneficial for chronic conditions, improving general health and helping behavioural problems. They are not suitable for a serious infection, acute condition or for emergency situations.

Some veterinarians practise complementary therapies themselves, while others will refer you to specialists. By law, some treatments can only be practised by or in conjunction with a veterinarian. Always check the credentials of a practitioner before they work on your pet. Do not use unqualified or unlicensed practitioners, or a therapist that is not trained to work with animals.

ACUPUNCTURE

Veterinary acupuncture has been practised for thousands of years. It involves inserting needles into the animal to stimulate the flow of energy around the body. The scientific explanation for its apparent effectiveness is that it promotes the production of painkilling endorphins in the body. Acupuncture is often recommended for cats who suffer from chronic pain, arthritis, asthma and nerve problems.

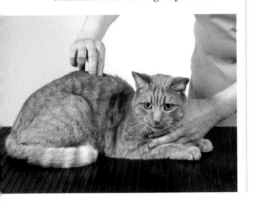

Left: Chiropractic medicine is a growing area of expertise, and may be helpful for joint problems.

CHIROPRACTIC MEDICINE

This hands-on therapy involves gentle manipulation of the spine and joints. Veterinary chiropractors should be trained in feline anatomy. Conditions said to respond to this therapy include arthritis, back and joint problems, and lameness.

OSTEOPATHY

Like chiropractic medicine, this is a hands-on therapy. Practitioners work with the soft tissues and joints, and the aim is to correct any misalignments that are causing pain. Lameness, joint problems, muscle strain and arthritis may be relieved by osteopathy.

HOMEOPATHY

The theory behind homeopathy is that 'like cures like', so a substance that would cause certain symptoms can also stimulate the body's natural defences and cure them. Animal substances, minerals and plants are all used, and the remedies are diluted many many times. Homeopathy is used for conditions such as allergy, skin problems, gastro-intestinal problems and respiratory disorders.

HERBAL MEDICINE

Herbs have long been used in healing and are the basis of many modern drugs. Herbalism may be used for serious conditions such as heart and circulatory conditions, digestive complaints, skin diseases, and muscle and joint problems. Cats are highly sensitive to many substances that are tolerated by people and dogs, so adverse effects are a concern. Avoid unlicensed herbal remedies.

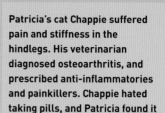

CASE HISTORY
Acupuncture for cats

Patricia's cat Chappie suffered pain and stiffness in the hindlegs. His veterinarian diagnosed osteoarthritis, and prescribed anti-inflammatories and painkillers. Chappie hated taking pills, and Patricia found it stressful to give them to him.

- -

With her veterinarian's support, Patricia took her cat to a specialist centre for veterinary acupuncture. She was concerned that Chappie might find the treatment stressful, but he had no problem accepting the insertion of needles, and even fell asleep at the session. The acupuncture had a beneficial effect, giving Chappie relief from his pain, and he was soon able to discontinue the pills. Patricia was highly relieved, and took Chappie for monthly acupuncture treatment to relieve his pain thereafter.

Pregnancy and birth

Pregnancy and birth is usually straightforward for cats, but you should take some sensible precautions to help ensure that your cat – and her kittens – are healthy. Take your cat for a check-up at the veterinarian's when you think she is pregnant.

Many unwanted kittens are born every year, so it is best not to breed from your cat unless you are sure that you can place the kittens. Your cat should be at least a year old, fully vaccinated, and free from viral diseases such as FeLV and FIV. If possible, the tom should also be tested and be vaccinated. If your cat is a pedigree, discuss your plans with a breeder. Some cat breeds have genetic health problems that have to to be taken into account when choosing a mate.

Many cats, especially indoor–outdoor ones, get pregnant accidentally. You may not realize that your cat is pregnant until her belly swells at about five weeks. The first sign is pinker, larger nipples after three weeks. Pregnancy usually lasts nine weeks in all.

PRENATAL CARE

If you suspect your cat is pregnant, take her to the veterinarian's for a check-up. Pregnant queens need a nourishing diet, and will usually need to eat more after the fifth week of pregnancy. Your cat should continue to have monthly worming and flea treatments, but check that they are safe for use during pregnancy. Don't give your cat any supplements or medications unless they are advised by your veterinarian.

Left: **A cat's pregnancy lasts nine weeks. There is little visible sign until the fifth week, which is also when the cat starts to modify her usual behaviour.**

About two weeks before the birth, your cat will become restless as she searches for a birthing spot. Place a large cardboard box, with one side cut down, in a quiet, well-ventilated room where she will not be disturbed. Line the box with paper that can be shredded. Hopefully your cat will 'queen' here, but she may prefer to find her own spot. Keep a close eye on her in the days before the birth in case she chooses somewhere unsafe.

Above: **A litter can mean anything from two to eight kittens, but the norm for most queens is three to five.**

THE BIRTH

A cat calls, and licks the vaginal area, before the births. Milk may discharge from her nipples. Keep a close eye on her, but do not interfere. The kittens will be born at intervals, and the mother will usually lick each one clean, eating the amniotic sac and the afterbirth (which contains important nutrients). If she doesn't do this, tear the sac with clean hands and rub the kitten gently with a clean flannel. Holding the kitten head-down will help drain fluid from its airways if it does not start to breathe.

The mother should bite through the cord. If not, soak some thread and scissors in antiseptic, then tie the thread around the umbilical cord about three centimetres (a generous inch) from the body and cut off the cord on the placenta side with the scissors. Put the kitten close to the mother's nipple so it can suckle.

Call the veterinarian in the following circumstances: if a pregnant cat seems to be going into labour earlier than 60 days; if she strains for 30 minutes without producing a kitten; if a kitten appears to be stuck in the birth canal; if the mother shows little interest in her offspring; if she appears weak or sick; if you see an odorous, green discharge or bright red bleeding; or if you have not seen a placenta for each kitten born.

Basic kitten care

A queen will usually take good care of her kittens. Providing for the mother is your main task – but take time to enjoy the new baby cats, too. Handle the kittens from about two weeks to accustom them to human contact.

Kittens feed shortly after the birth, and then at frequent intervals. When they finish suckling, the mother licks their rears to stimulate excretion, and will clean up any waste until the kittens start to eat solid food. Change the bedding regularly to help keep the nest clean. So long as the mother and kittens seem healthy, you should leave them alone for the first two weeks, other than to make regular checks. It is best to avoid handling the kittens at this time. Contact your veterinarian if the kittens are not feeding well, or if the mother seems weak or agitated.

THE EARLY DAYS

A kitten's eyes open after about one week, and hearing and vision mature from two weeks. They become more mobile at three weeks, and enjoy exploring their surroundings; make sure these are kittenproof and safe (see pages 76–7).

Offer a specially formulated kitten food from three weeks. Ordinary cat food is not suitable for cats less than one year old. If you choose a dry food, soak it in water or milk substitute, then mash well. Give small amounts four to six times a day, gradually increasing the quantity.

Below: **Your kittens will have lots of fun playing with their littermates, but claws and teeth will soon become sharp enough to do real damage.**

Cut down to three or four meals a day by six weeks. By eight weeks, the kitten should be fully weaned. Make sure your kittens always have access to fresh water.

PREPARING YOUR KITTENS FOR NEW HOMES

Start handling your kittens regularly from two weeks. Cats that are not held between three and seven weeks shy from human contact later on. Plan the kittens' worming programme with your veterinarian: kittens need to be wormed for roundworms at about four weeks, and then every two weeks. The kittens should receive their first innoculations at about eight weeks, and they should not be allowed outside until they have been vaccinated.

Provide a litter tray from about three weeks. The mother will teach the kittens how to use it. If she doesn't, place the kittens on the litter tray after each feed.

FINDING HOMES

Always ask a prospective owner how your kitten will be cared for. Check whether this person has owned animals before and ask if there are

Above: **Unless you plan to let your cat have another litter, discuss neutering with your veterinarian before the kittens are weaned.**

young children or other animals in the home. Consider whether this person will care properly for your kitten. If the prospective owner is working, consider whether the house will be empty during the day and bear in mind that your kittens will be happier if they are settled with a littermate. Be prepared to advise on kitten care if the prospective owner has not had a cat before.

BASIC INSTINCT **Why a mother cat moves her kittens**

A mother cat may move her kittens within days of the birth if she feels unsafe. She will pick up each kitten by the scruff of its neck, moving the litter one at a time to a new home (it is best not to interfere with this process).

At around three weeks, she usually moves her kittens again. This is almost certainly an instinctive behaviour: in the wild, she would move her kittens closer to the hunting ground as she prepares to teach them to hunt for themselves.

The older cat

As a cat ages, its health gradually declines and it starts to slow down. This is natural, but there is much you can do to ensure that your cat enjoys a comfortable old age. Keep a close eye on it and take it for regular veterinary check-ups.

A cat is considered a senior citizen from about the age of eight, and geriatric at about fourteen. As a cat ages, it starts to slow down – much as humans do – by spending more time sleeping and having slower reactions. Your cat's temperament changes, too. It is likely to find change more difficult, so you should avoid disrupting its routine. And it may have more need for you – older cats often yowl at night if left alone. A kind owner will give an elderly cat lots of affection and attention.

GENERAL CHANGES

Ageing cats naturally become less mobile. They find it harder to jump up to a favourite spot and may struggle to groom as they used to. Older cats benefit from more regular grooming sessions, and are likely to need their nails clipping more often. An older cat cannot regulate its temperature as efficiently and will seek out warm places to sleep. Put its bed closer to a heat source and don't allow older indoor-outdoor cats to go out on cold days.

Above: **A cat becomes quieter and less active in its final years, but can still be a rewarding companion.**

Hearing and vision also decline. A blind cat can manage reasonably well in the home, but you should avoid moving furniture unless necessary. Deafness puts your cat more at risk of traffic accidents, so it should be kept indoors. See your veterinarian if you notice any disorientation, changes to the eyes, or lack of responsiveness when you call.

DIET

Elderly cats are naturally less active so they put on weight easily. It is important to adjust your cat's diet, and feed it a specially formulated food that takes account of its special nutritional needs (older cats need more fibre and vitamins and less protein and fat). Your veterinarian may also recommend a special diet or supplements to keep your cat in good condition.

An older cat is also subject to constipation and incontinence. Seek veterinary help at the first sign of toileting problems; they are easier to treat early on.

Make sure that your cat always has fresh water available. If your cat starts to drink more, this could indicate diabetes, hyperthyroidism or kidney failure.

HEALTH PROBLEMS

Health problems may manifest themselves as changes in behaviour, appetite or toileting habits. It is important to keep a close eye on your cat and report any unusual changes to your veterinarian.

Older cats are more susceptible to a range of health problems, including

CHECKLIST
How old is my cat in human terms?

Cat	Human
1 month	6 months
3 months	2–3 years
5 months	8–9 years
6 months	14 years
1 year	18 years
2 years	25 years
3 years	30 years
4 years	35 years
5 years	40 years
6 years	42–3 years
7 years	45 years
8 years	48 years
9 years	55 years
10 years	60 years
11 years	62 years
12 years	65 years
13 years	68 years
14 years	72 years
15 years	74 years
16 years	76 years
17 years	78 years
18 years	80 years

arthritis, tooth and gum problems, kidney disease, high blood pressure, heart disease and hyperthyroidism. Reporting symptoms quickly to a veterinarian is key to prolonging your cat's life. In addition, take your cat for twice-yearly check-ups, and make sure its vaccinations and parasite treatments are maintained.

When the end comes

Cats do not live as long as people, so most pet owners have to say goodbye to their pets sooner or later. This is a difficult event and you need to prepare for it. Allow yourself time to mourn the loss of your pet and seek help if emotions are overwhelming.

If your cat dies suddenly it can be a great shock, and you will need time to grieve. If, however, you make the decision to put your cat down, you have time to prepare yourself – but that does not make losing your cat any less painful.

WHEN TO LET GO

You will naturally want to keep your cat as long as possible. But if your cat is in constant pain or distress, then the kindest thing may be to end its suffering. Your cat's quality of life will decline if it is unable to move, eat or drink properly, or if it has trouble breathing. Your veterinarian is there to help you to make the decision when the time comes, and to answer any questions you may have.

THE PROCEDURE

Once you decide to have your cat put to sleep, choose a time when the surgery is not busy to have it done. Discuss with your veterinarian what you want to do with your cat's body. On the day, you will be asked to sign a consent form. The veterinarian will

shave a patch of fur from the foreleg, and inject it with an overdose of anaesthetic. The cat falls asleep, and its breathing and heartbeat stop soon after.

Many owners stay with their cat, so that it has a familiar presence during its last moments. However, if you are likely to become upset, this may make your cat stressed.

Below: **Many people like to mark their cat's resting place with a gravestone, plaque or perhaps a special plant. Another option is to make a donation to an animal charity.**

Above: **Most veterinarians understand the pain that an owner undergoes when putting a cat to sleep, and will discuss any questions that you might have sympathetically.**

AFTER THE PROCEDURE

Your veterinarian can have your cat cremated in a pet crematorium, or you can arrange this yourself. If you want your cat's ashes returned to you, you will need to ensure that your cat has an individual cremation.

Another option is to bury your cat, either in a pet cemetery or in your garden. Do check local ordinances first to ensure that this is legal. The hole should be at least one metre (3 ft) deep, and a heavy object should be placed on top to deter predators. Make sure it is well away from natural water courses.

DEALING WITH GRIEF

Grief is normal after losing your cat. Allow yourself time to mourn, and seek help if your emotions are overwhelming. Pet bereavement counselling is offered by some charities, and you may also be able to access this through your doctor. Cat owners often worry that their feelings will be ridiculed. It can be helpful to talk to other animal lovers, who are likely to understand your feelings at losing a treasured companion.

If you have children, it is best to talk plainly about what has happened, and to explain clearly that the cat has died. Avoid using the term 'gone to sleep', which can be confusing for them.

Useful contacts

UK

CHARITIES AND ADVICE

Blue Cross
Shilton Road
Burford
Oxon OX18 4PF
01993 822651
www.bluecross.org.uk

Cats Protection
National Cat Centre
Chelwood Gate
Haywards Heath
Sussex RH17 7TT
03000 12 12 12 (national helpline)
www.cats.org.uk

Feline Advisory Bureau (FAB)
Taeselbury
High Street
Tisbury
Wiltshire SP3 6LD
01747 871872
www.fabcats.org

Royal Society for the Prevention of Cruelty to Animals
RSPCA Enquiries Service
Wilberforce Way
Southwater
Horsham
West Sussex RH13 9RS
0300 1234 555
www.rspca.org.uk

LOST CATS

Petlog
The Kennel Club
4A Alton House
Gatehouse Way
Aylesbury
Bucks HP19 8XU
0844 463 3999
www.thekennelclub.org.uk/ petlog

UK National Missing Pets Register
16 Richmond Avenue
Thornton-Cleveleys
Lancashire
FY5 2BP
www.nationalpetregister.org

VETERINARY ASSOCIATIONS

British Veterinary Association
7 Mansfield Street
London W1G 9NQ
020 7636 6541
www.bva.co.uk

BREED REGISTRIES

The Governing Council of the Cat Fancy
5 King's Castle Business Park

The Drove
Bridgwater
Somerset TA6 4AG
01278 427575
www.gccfcats.org

USA

CHARITIES AND ADVICE

American Society for the Prevention of Cruelty to Animals
424 E. 92nd St
New York
NY 10128-6804
212-876-7700
www.aspca.org

The Humane Society of the United States
2100 L Street, NW
Washington, DC 20037
202-452-1100
www.humanesociety.org

LOST CATS
Lost Pet USA
PO Box 33
Kenilworth, IL 60043
www.lostpetusa.net

American Kennel Club Companion Animal Recovery
AKC CAR
8051 Arco Corporate Drive
Suite 200
Raleigh, NC 27617-3900
800-252-7894
www.akccar.org

VETERINARY ASSOCIATIONS
American Association of Feline Practitioners
390 Amwell Road
Suite 403
Hillsborough, NJ 08844
800-874-0498
www.catvets.com

American Veterinary Medical Association
1931 North Meacham Road
Suite 100
Schaumburg

IL 60173-4360
800-248-286
www.avma.org

BREED REGISTRIES
Cat Fanciers Association
1805 Atlantic Avenue
PO Box 1005
Manasquan
NJ 08736-0805
732-528-9797
www.cfainc.org

American Cat Fanciers Association
PO Box 1949
Nixa
MO 65714-1949
417-725-1530
www.acfacat.com

AUSTRALIA
CHARITIES AND ADVICE
Cat Protection Society of Victoria
PO Box 257
Greensborough
VIC 3088
03 9434 7155
www.catprotection.com.au

Cat Protection Society of NSW
103 Enmore Road
Newtown
NSW 2042
02 9519 7201
www.catprotection.org.au

RSPCA Australia Inc
PO Box 265
Deakin West
ACT 2600
02 6282 8300
www.rspca.org.au

LOST CATS
National Pet Register
2 Gracie Street
North Melbourne
VIC 3051
1300 734 738
www.petregister.com.au

VETERINARY ASSOCIATIONS
The Australian Veterinary Association Ltd
Unit 40
6 Herbert Street
St Leonards
NSW 2065
02 9431 5000
www.ava.com.au

BREED REGISTRIES
Australian Cat Federation (Inc)
PO Box 331
Port Adelaide BC
SA 5015
08 8449 5880
www.acf.asn.au

Index

Author

Catherine Davidson got her first cat at the age of ten and has loved felines ever since. She is the author of numerous reference titles including *Why Does My Cat Do That?* and *Cats: A Guide to Cat Breeds and their Fascinating History.*

Picture Credits

Quercus Publishing Plc
21 Bloomsbury Square
London
WC1A 2NS

First published in 2010

Copyright © Quercus Publishing Plc 2010

This edition produced by Ivy Contract

Text by Catherine Davidson

A catalogue record of this book is available from the British Library

UK and associated territories
ISBN: 978 1 84866 048 9

USA and associated territories
ISBN: 978 1 84866 075 5

Printed and bound in China

10 9 8 7 6 5 4 3 2 1